MONONUCLEOSIS

Anthrax

Cholera

HIV/AIDS

Influenza

Lyme Disease

Malaria

Mononucleosis

Polio

Syphilis

Toxic Shock Syndrome

Tuberculosis

Typhoid Fever

DEADLY DISEASES AND EPIDEMICS

MONONUCLEOSIS

Janet Decker

CONSULTING EDITOR
I. Edward Alcamo
Distinguished Teaching Professor of Microbiology,
SUNY Farmingdale

FOREWORD BY
David Heymann
World Health Organization

CHELSEA HOUSE
P U B L I S H E R S
A Haights Cross Communications Company
Philadelphia

Dedication

We dedicate the books in the DEADLY DISEASES AND EPIDEMICS series to Ed Alcamo, whose wit, charm, intelligence, and commitment to biology education were second to none.

CHELSEA HOUSE PUBLISHERS

VP, NEW PRODUCT DEVELOPMENT Sally Cheney
DIRECTOR OF PRODUCTION Kim Shinners
CREATIVE MANAGER Takeshi Takahashi
MANUFACTURING MANAGER Diann Grasse

Staff for Mononucleosis

ASSOCIATE EDITOR Beth Reger
PRODUCTION EDITOR Megan Emery
PHOTO EDITOR Sarah Bloom
SERIES DESIGNER Terry Mallon
COVER DESIGNER Keith Trego
LAYOUT 21st Century Publishing and Communications, Inc.

A Haights Cross Communications ✦ Company

http://www.chelseahouse.com

First Printing

1 3 5 7 9 8 6 4 2

Library of Congress Cataloging-in-Publication Data

Decker, Janet M.
    Mononucleosis/Janet Decker.
        p. cm.—(Deadly diseases and epidemics)
Includes index.
Contents: Infectious mononucleosis and the epstein-barr virus (ebv)—The
discovery of epstein-barr virus—The life of epstein-barr virus—Immune system
response to epstein-barr virus—Signs and symptoms—Ebv transmission and
latent infection—Diagnosis of infectious mononucleosis—Treatments for
infectious mononucleosis—Ebv and cancer—Ebv and other diseases.
    ISBN 0-7910-7700-4
    1. Mononucleosis—Juvenile literature. [1. Mononucleosis. 2. Diseases.]
I. Title. II. Series.
RC147.G6D435 2003
616.9'1122—dc22

                                                                2003020143

Table of Contents

Foreword

In the 1960s, infectious diseases—which had terrorized generations— were tamed. Building on a century of discoveries, the leading killers of Americans both young and old were being prevented with new vaccines or cured with new medicines. The risk of death from pneumonia, tuberculosis, meningitis, influenza, whooping cough, and diphtheria declined dramatically. New vaccines lifted the fear that summer would bring polio, and a global campaign was approaching the global eradication of smallpox. New pesticides like DDT cleared mosquitoes from homes and fields, thus reducing the incidence of malaria which was present in the southern United States and a leading killer of children worldwide. New technologies produced safe drinking water and removed the risk of cholera and other water-borne diseases. Science seemed unstoppable. Disease seemed destined to almost disappear.

But the euphoria of the 1960s has evaporated.

Microbes fight back. Those causing diseases like TB and malaria evolved resistance to cheap and effective drugs. The mosquito evolved the ability to defuse pesticides. New diseases emerged, including AIDS, Legionnaires, and Lyme disease. And diseases which have not been seen in decades re-emerge, as the hantavirus did in the Navajo Nation in 1993. Technology itself actually created new health risks. The global transportation network, for example, meant that diseases like West Nile virus could spread beyond isolated regions in distant countries and quickly become global threats. Even modern public health protections sometimes failed, as they did in Milwaukee, Wisconsin, in 1993 which resulted in 400,000 cases of the digestive system illness cryptosporidiosis. And, more recently, the threat from smallpox, a disease completely eradicated, has returned along with other potential bioterrorism weapons such as anthrax.

The lesson is that the fight against infectious diseases will never end.

In this constant struggle against disease, we as individuals have a weapon that does not require vaccines or drugs, the warehouse of knowledge. We learn from the history of science that "modern" beliefs can be wrong. In this series of books, for example, you will learn that diseases like syphilis were once thought to be caused by eating potatoes. The invention of the microscope set science on the right path. There are more positive lessons from history. For example, smallpox was eliminated by vaccinating everyone who had come in contact with an infected person. This "ring" approach to controlling smallpox is still the preferred method for confronting a smallpox outbreak should the disease be intentionally reintroduced.

At the same time, we are constantly adding new drugs, new vaccines, and new information to the warehouse. Recently, the entire human genome was decoded. So too was the genome of the parasite that causes malaria. Perhaps by looking at the microbe and the victim through the lens of genetics we will to be able to discover new ways of fighting malaria, still the leading killer of children in many countries.

Because of the knowledge gained about such diseases as AIDS, entire new classes of anti-retroviral drugs have been developed. But resistance to all these drugs has already been detected, so we know that AIDS drug development must continue.

Education, experimentation, and the discoveries which grow out of them are the best tools to protect health. Opening this book may put you on the path of discovery. I hope so, because new vaccines, new antibiotics, new technologies and, most importantly, new scientists are needed now more than ever if we are to remain on the winning side of this struggle with microbes.

David Heymann
Executive Director
Communicable Diseases Section
World Health Organization
Geneva, Switzerland

1

Introduction: Infectious Mononucleosis and Epstein-Barr Virus

INFECTIOUS MONONUCLEOSIS: THE "KISSING DISEASE"

Stacy awoke with the worst sore throat she had ever had. She had been feeling tired for the past few days, but now she felt feverish and the glands in her neck were swollen. She felt too sick to get out of bed. For the next few days, her throat continued to feel sore and her glands were swollen and tender. Every afternoon, her temperature would rise to 101°F, and she felt exhausted even though all she did was sleep.

Stacy decided to see her doctor, who saw that Stacy's tonsils were swollen (Figure 1.1) and her throat was very red. Stacy's heart and lungs sounded normal, and she did not have a rash. The doctor noted that Stacy's abdomen was a little tender and could feel that her spleen was somewhat enlarged. Suspecting that Stacy had a classic case of infectious mononucleosis, the doctor took a blood sample to confirm the diagnosis.

Infectious mononucleosis (mono) is a disease caused by the Epstein-Barr **virus** (EBV). **EBV** infects the cells of the throat and the **immune system.** The blood of someone with mono contains high numbers of white blood cells called mononuclear cells. Mononuclear cells also make the tonsils and spleen swollen. A person with a swollen spleen must avoid any extra pressure to the area; even a moderate blow can cause it to rupture. The immune system causes **fever** and fatigue as it attacks the virus. Antibiotics are not effective against viruses, including EBV.

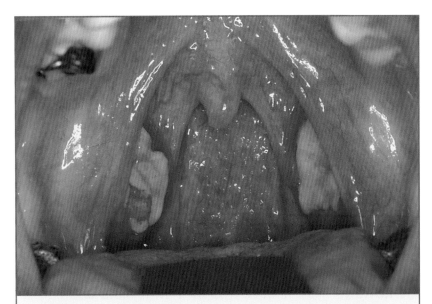

Figure 1.1 Swollen tonsils, shown here, are a common symptom of mononucleosis. When the Epstein-Barr virus infects the cells of the throat, white blood cells called mononuclear cells are recruited to fight the disease. These cells can cause the tonsils to swell.

Usually the sore throat lasts only a few days and can be treated with pain relievers. The tired feeling lasts for several weeks as the immune system fights the virus. People with mononucleosis can gradually resume normal activities, but they must generally avoid sports for three to four weeks. That is because the swollen spleen could be ruptured by even moderate pressure, causing serious internal bleeding.

People infected with EBV have the virus in their saliva, where it can be passed to other people by kissing or sharing utensils (this is why mononucleosis is often termed "the kissing disease" by high school and college students). Mononucleosis cannot be transmitted through the air. Many infected people, especially small children, do not have any symptoms when they get mononucleosis. When teens and young adults become infected, they usually have fever, swollen glands, and fatigue.

Once people have been infected, they will always have the virus in their bodies and can "shed" it in their saliva, even if they do not feel sick. Most people with mono recover completely and do not get symptoms again.

EBV AND BONE MARROW TRANSPLANTS

Like Stacy, Frank also became infected with EBV, but his experience was quite different. Frank had received a bone marrow transplant to treat **leukemia**, a cancer of the white blood cells. He received radiation and drugs to kill the leukemia cells, and his blood-forming cells were replaced with bone marrow from a donor. As new white blood cells were produced by the donor bone marrow, abnormal rapidly dividing cells appeared in his blood. The cells were abnormal because they were infected with EBV (Figure 1.2).

EBV infection is a much more serious disease in someone like Frank whose immune system is weakened by cancer or the antirejection drugs given to transplant patients. Nearly everyone has been infected with EBV by the time they reach adulthood, and EBV can remain hidden in blood cells for life. Transplanted bone marrow can contain EBV-infected cells that transmit the virus to the bone marrow recipient. Because the immune system cannot fight the virus effectively, virus-infected cells can multiply in the blood. These cells can crowd out normal blood cells and can eventually be fatal. Strong antiviral drugs or white blood cells from a healthy person must be given to control the EBV infection.

ONE VIRUS, MANY IDENTITIES

Both Stacy and Frank were infected with EBV. More than 95% of people worldwide are infected. The virus can cause a range of illnesses. Many people are infected when they are children and have no symptoms or very minor ones. Other people, like Stacy, acquire EBV as adolescents and suffer the classic symptoms of infectious mononucleosis: sore throat, swollen

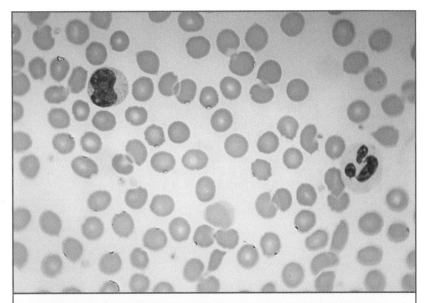

Figure 1.2 The Epstein-Barr virus, which causes mononucleosis, infects the white blood cells and causes them to become abnormally shaped. In the blood smear shown here, two large white blood cells (purple and white) can be seen among the red blood cells of an infected individual.

glands, and fatigue. Only a small number of people in the United States, all with weakened immune systems like Frank's, develop a life-threatening illness from EBV. In some parts of central Africa, children who are infected with EBV develop tumors of the jaw called **Burkitt's lymphoma**. In China and other parts of Southeast Asia, adults develop a cancer of the nose and mouth; their tumor cells carry EBV genes.

To understand how one virus can cause so many illnesses, it is necessary to examine the virus itself, how it affects the body, how it is detected, and how it is treated. It is also important to learn about the history of viruses in general and the history of Epstein-Barr virus. Then, the relationship between EBV and other diseases, such as the ones mentioned above, will become clear.

2

The Discovery of Epstein-Barr Virus

HISTORY OF VIRUSES

More than 400 different viruses cause diseases in humans, ranging from colds and diarrhea to AIDS and cancer. Currently in the United States, viruses are responsible for 80% of acute infections, infections which last only a few days to perhaps a month and cause noticeable symptoms. Viruses have been infecting humans for as long as humans have existed. In fact, viruses are probably older than humans. Viruses that infect bacteria have probably existed almost as long as bacteria have. Viruses can also infect animals, plants, and insects.

Clear signs of what are now known to be viral infections, including smallpox, genital warts, and polio, can be seen in Egyptian mummies. Descriptions of viral diseases can be found in medical texts written thousands of years ago. In the sixteenth century, the smallpox virus was brought to the Americas by infected Spanish explorers. The native inhabitants of Mexico had no immunity to smallpox and many died, allowing the others to be conquered by the Spanish. Yellow fever virus killed 20,000 people in 1881–82 and caused the French to abandon digging the Panama Canal. The great influenza epidemic of 1918 and 1919 killed millions of people worldwide.

In seventeenth-century Holland, tulip viruses caused the flowers to display brightly colored patterns (Figure 2.1). The presence of the virus in some cells of the tulip flower blocked the cells' ability to produce certain colored pigments. Infected cells appeared a different color than uninfected cells. For example, infected cells might be yellow and uninfected

Figure 2.1 Tulip viruses in Holland cause unevenly colored flowers, as in this picture. When the virus infects certain cells in the plant, it blocks the cells' ability to produce certain colored pigments. The result is a multicolored tulip. The virus does not harm the flowers.

cells might be red. The pattern of red and yellow would differ from flower to flower, depending on which cells were infected with the virus. In this case, the virus did not kill the infected cells but changed their appearance in a way that was not harmful to the plant and was very beneficial to the tulip farmers. Tulip growers were so excited about the new varieties that they pledged their homes and even their daughters in marriage to obtain a single tulip bulb. Speculation on the tulip bulb market nearly ruined the economy of Holland.

Viruses are still being discovered or are appearing in new regions of the world. The Ebola virus emerged from the African jungle in 1967 to kill more than 90% of the people it infected. **HIV** was recognized in the 1980s when it began attacking the immune systems of gay men in San Francisco and Los Angeles. The hantavirus was recognized as a cause of a serious respiratory infection in the American Southwest in 1993. In 1999, West Nile virus migrated to the United States in birds to cause outbreaks of mosquito-borne encephalitis in humans, birds, and horses. In the winter of 2003, life-threatening cases of pneumonia from Vietnam and China spread to Europe and Canada and slowed or in some cases stopped international travel to affected areas and closed schools and hospitals. The cause of severe acute respiratory syndrome (SARS) was identified as a new variant of a coronavirus. Known coronaviruses cause mild to moderate respiratory infections in humans and also can cause severe diseases in animals. In the spring of 2003, monkeypox, caused by a close relative of the smallpox virus, traveled from Africa to the United States in rats imported to be sold as pets. It infected pet prairie dogs and then their human owners, causing a blister-like skin rash.

Today we know a great deal about viruses and have sophisticated methods to diagnose infections and study virus biology. However, because viruses are so small and must be grown inside other living cells, viruses were the last of the microorganisms to be identified and understood. The study of viruses began just a little more than 100 years ago with a virus that was damaging tobacco leaves.

FILTERING A VIRUS

Antony van Leeuwenhoek, a Dutch fabric merchant who ground lenses as a hobby, first observed bacteria with his simple lenses in 1676. However, it was more than 200 years later before humans understood that infectious agents rather than bad air or the influence of the planets were responsible for many human and animal diseases. In 1876, Robert Koch proved that a bacterium caused anthrax by isolating the bacterium from a cow with anthrax, growing the bacterium in the laboratory in the absence of other bacteria, and then causing the same disease by injecting the bacterium into a mouse. Koch's Postulates, the "rules" for demonstrating that a particular bacterium caused a particular disease, became widely accepted by other scientists and physicians.

However, for some diseases the infectious agent could not be isolated and grown in the laboratory. Louis Pasteur developed a rabies **vaccine** without ever isolating and identifying the rabies virus. One of Pasteur's assistants, Charles Chamberland, invented a porcelain filter with pores so small that bacteria could not pass through it. For some diseases, however, the infectious agent did pass through the Chamberland filter. Bacteriologists could stain bacteria with dyes and observe them under the microscope, but the infectious agents that passed through Chamberland's filter were invisible even under the microscope. In 1887, a surgeon and bacteriologist at the University of Edinburgh saw some very small red dots about one-fourth the size of a bacterial cell in material from a smallpox vaccination sore. John Buist was the first person to see a virus, although he thought the red dots were actually bacterial **spores**. Spores are thick-walled structures that some bacteria make to survive harsh environmental conditions. However, he could not grow the agent in the lab and gave up those studies.

In 1892, Dmitry Ivanovsky was studying tobacco mosaic disease in Russia (Figures 2.2a and 2.2b). Tobacco plants that

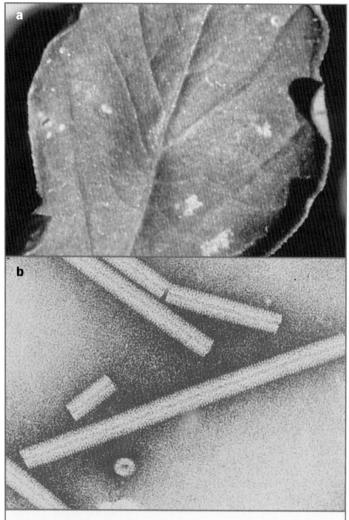

Figure 2.2 The tobacco mosaic virus causes tobacco leaves to develop pale spots, as in the top photograph. The virus itself is long and cylindrical (bottom).

contracted mosaic disease would become stunted, and their leaves would become so covered in pale spots that they could not be used for cigar wrappings. Tobacco farmers all across Europe lost a great deal of money because of tobacco mosaic disease. Ivanovsky crushed leaves from the mottled plants and passed the liquid he obtained through a Chamberland filter. He expected that the filter would trap the infectious agent, but he was wrong. When Ivanovsky put some of the sap that had passed through the filter onto the leaves of healthy tobacco plants, they soon developed tobacco mosaic disease. Ivanovsky suspected that either the filter was defective and had allowed a very small bacterium to pass through or that a toxin molecule rather than a living cell caused mosaic disease.

Meanwhile in Delft, the home of Antony van Leeuwenhoek, a Dutch botanist named Martinus Beijerinck (BUY-er-ink) was also studying tobacco mosaic disease. He had not heard of Ivanovsky's results because they had not been published outside of Russia. Beijerinck also found something in the filtered sap from diseased tobacco leaves that could infect healthy plants. From careful measurements, he showed that the agent was reproducing in the tobacco leaves even though it could not be grown in the laboratory. The agent could survive in sap for three months and still be infectious. It could also survive treatment with formalin and alcohol, chemicals that kill bacteria. However, when Beijerinck heated his sap to 194°C (381.2°F), a temperature that would kill bacteria, but not bacterial spores, his agent did not survive. The agent was something new, not a typical bacterium or a bacterial spore. Beijerinck called it a *contagium vivum fluidum*—a contagious living fluid. He suggested that the particle might have to reproduce in living cells, and he named it a virus, the Latin word for poison.

Beijerinck published his results in 1898. When Ivanovsky heard of Beijerinck's experiments, he announced that he had already made the same discovery and concluded that the mosaic disease agent must be multiplying in the tobacco leaves, even though he had originally said that the agent was probably a toxin. Rather than compete, Beijerinck stopped his tobacco mosaic virus work and went onto other projects (see box on page 18).

Neither of these early virus hunters had a clear vision of the nature of tobacco mosaic virus (**TMV**).

Other viruses were soon discovered: foot-and-mouth disease virus in 1898 by Friedrich Löffler and Paul Frosch, yellow fever virus in 1901 by Walter Reed and James Carroll,

MARTINUS BEIJERINCK

Martinus Beijerinck was one of the early microbiologists whose findings helped to define the new field of microbiology. At the age of 34, he became a microbiologist at the Netherlands Yeast and Alcohol Manufactory in Delft. Unlike many microbiologists of the time who followed Pasteur and Koch in the study of human disease, Beijerinck concentrated on plant and industrial microbiology. He continued these interests as a professor of microbiology at the Polytechnical University in Delft.

In addition to his studies on tobacco mosaic virus, Beijerinck studied many other areas of microbiology. By isolating bacteria from the nodules of leguminous plants, he demonstrated that they could convert atmospheric nitrogen into nitrogen-containing molecules used by plants and animals. He studied alcohol fermentation in yeasts and the ability of some bacteria to extract energy from sulfur compounds. He also characterized the microbes that are responsible for the production of kefir, a fermented milk beverage popular in Eastern Europe. He developed enrichment cultures that allowed him to encourage the growth of certain bacteria in the laboratory. He was one of the earliest scientists to propose that the hereditary characteristics of an organism corresponded to its ability to produce certain enzymes.

Beijerinck received many honors during his career, but when he was forced to retire at age 70, he left Delft and saw few people during the last 10 years of his life. Many of his students went on to make important contributions in microbiology and biotechnology.

and a bacteria-infecting virus (a **bacteriophage**) in 1917 by Felix d'Hérelle. In the 1930s, the electron microscope was invented, allowing scientists to see virus particles.

One of the problems associated with studying viruses was obtaining enough viruses, especially from infected humans. A human virus was first grown outside the body by Ernest Goodpasture and Alice Woodruff, who grew the smallpox virus in fertilized chicken eggs. Wendell Stanley crystallized TMV and reported that it was composed of protein. A few years later, Frederick Bawden and Norman Pirie discovered that TMV also contained a tiny amount of RNA. It was not until the 1950s, when James Watson and Francis Crick discovered the structure of **DNA** and it became possible to grow viruses in tissue culture, that virology really blossomed as a science.

DISCOVERING BURKITT'S LYMPHOMA

Denis Burkitt had traveled with his wife and three daughters from Scotland to Kampala, Uganda, to become a medical missionary with the Colonial Medical Service. As a surgeon at Mulago Hospital in 1957, Dr. Burkitt began to notice children with tumors of the jaw. He operated to remove the tumors, but the children usually died. When he saw a five-year-old boy with tumors on both sides of his jaw, and then within a few weeks, treated a young girl with similar tumors in her jaw and in other parts of her body, he began to wonder about these children with cancer. Hospital records showed similar cases of tumors of the jaw and other parts of the body in children between the ages of two and fourteen, with most of the tumors occurring in children about the age of five.

Dr. Burkitt knew that cancer was rare in children; it was mostly a disease of older people. It was also unusual to find the same type of tumors in different organs; tumors usually affected a single organ. Dr. Burkitt asked pathologists at the nearby medical school to look at the children's tumors under the microscope. The jaw and organ tumors looked the same.

The tumors that Dr. Burkitt was seeing were lymphomas, solid tumors of the white blood cells. Half of the childhood cancers in the Kampala records were **lymphomas**. He found pictures and descriptions of similar tumors from the early 1800s, so he was not seeing a new cancer. In fact, old wooden carvings depicting jaw swellings indicated the tumors occurred much earlier than 1800.

George Oettlé, the director of the cancer research unit of the South African Institute for Medical Research in Johannesburg, came to Kampala. When he saw the pictures of the children with tumors, Dr. Oettlé said that he had never seen such cancers at his research institute. Dr. Burkitt decided to try to find out about these tumors that occurred in some areas of Africa and not other parts. He got a government grant to print and circulate 1,200 leaflets with pictures of children with jaw tumors to government and mission doctors through-out Africa.

After three years, Dr. Burkitt had received more than 300 replies. He saw that the lymphomas occurred in a band that stretched across Africa between 10 degrees north and 10 degrees south of the equator. The lymphoma band trailed down the east coast of Africa to the border of Mozambique and South Africa, then stopped. Within that five million square mile area, there were regions without tumors, most at altitudes higher than 5,000 feet above sea level. Dr. Burkitt called his studies "geographical biopsy." It was a new way to study cancer.

The northern border of the "lymphoma belt" was the Sahara Desert. Because revolutions were occurring in the western and southern regions, Dr. Burkitt decided to travel through eastern Africa from Kenya to South Africa.

In 1961, Burkitt and two other doctors traveled 10,000 miles through 12 countries. They visited as many hospitals as they could, asking about children with lymphomas. By the time they returned to Kampala, they had visited 57 hospitals and had seen more than 200 children with tumors. They had covered land ranging from 1,000 to 5,000 feet above sea level, and they had confirmed that South Africa had no cases of Burkitt's lymphoma.

Dr. Burkitt studied the pattern of pins marking cases of lymphoma on the map pinned to his wall. The pattern was more complicated than he had expected. Occurrence of lymphoma was dependent on altitude, temperature, and rainfall. An entomologist from the East African Virus Research Institute, who was a friend of Dr. Burkitt's, supplied a possible answer. Alexander Haddow suggested that the lymphoma maps corresponded to the habitat of the insect that carried sleeping sickness and yellow fever. Could insects also carry cancer?

DENIS PARSONS BURKITT

Denis Burkitt was born in Northern Ireland. As a boy, he lost an eye in a fight at school. He grew up planning to become an engineer like his father, who was also an ornithologist who studied the life of the robin. Denis was a poor student until he changed his studies from engineering to medicine. He graduated from Trinity College in Dublin and trained as a surgeon in Edinburgh, Scotland.

Burkitt wanted to become a medical missionary like his uncle, but his first application to the Colonial Medical Service was rejected because he had only one eye and, at age 30, he was considered too old. After serving in the Royal Army Medical Corps in Africa during Wolrd War II, Burkitt again applied to the Colonial Medical Service and was accepted. He served in Uganda from 1946 to 1964, during which time he mapped the occurrence of Burkitt's lymphoma.

Dr. Burkitt ended his career in London, studying the effects of diet on disease. Noting the differences between the African and European diets, Burkitt became convinced that the characteristically low-fiber diet of Western countries contributed to some of the more common medical maladies of Europe, such as gallstones, appendicitis, diabetes, and heart disease.

LINKING EBV TO MONONUCLEOSIS

Denis Burkitt could not do the laboratory research needed to solve the problem, but Dr. Anthony Epstein was ready to continue the work. He had attended a talk Burkitt gave in London and had become interested in the childhood tumors. He wanted to look for a virus in Burkitt's lymphoma cells. At that time, it was already known that viruses could cause tumors, but no one had found a tumor virus transmitted by an insect. Dr. Epstein arranged for tumor samples from Kampala to be flown to his lab at Middlesex Hospital in London. It took two years to grow the tumor cells in the lab. By that time Dr. Yvonne Barr had joined Epstein's lab, and they called the tumor cells EB cells. In 1964, using an electron microscope, they first saw the virus. They identified it as a previously unknown member of the herpesvirus family, related to the viruses that cause chicken pox and cold sores. However, no herpesvirus had ever been shown to cause cancer.

Dr. Epstein sent the Epstein-Barr virus (EBV) to the husband and wife virology team of Werner and Gertrude Henle at Philadelphia's Children's Hospital. The Henles had heard about Burkitt's lymphoma from a colleague, Dr. C. Everett Koop, who would later become surgeon general of the United States when President Ronald Reagan was in office. The Henles decided to look for antibodies to EBV in the blood of patients with Burkitt's lymphoma. They found that every child who had the lymphoma also had antibodies to EBV. Then, they tested children without Burkitt's lymphoma and found that they, too, had antibodies to EBV. Somehow EBV could infect children without causing an identified disease.

Levels of antibodies to EBV in children with Burkitt's lymphoma were about ten-fold higher than levels in healthy children. High EBV antibody levels were also found in adults with another kind of tumor, **nasopharyngeal carcinoma** (nase-oh-fare-in-GEE-al car-sin-oh-ma). This carcinoma is a tumor of the back of the nose and the roof of the mouth. It is found mostly in southern China, Southeast Asia, northern Africa, and Alaska. Nasopharyngeal carcinoma is very rare in the United States and Europe.

While the Henles pondered the antibody data, their lab technician called in sick. Elaine Hutkin had a fever, sore throat, and swollen glands in her neck, and she felt very tired. She continued to feel tired even after she returned to work six days later, and she developed a skin rash. The Henles tested her blood for antibodies to see if they could identify the cause of her illness. Elaine Hutkin had always tested negative for antibodies to EBV, but now her blood contained EBV-specific antibodies. She had become infected with EBV just about the time she had become sick. Elaine's doctor diagnosed her illness as infectious mononucleosis.

Infectious mononucleosis had been described in the late 1800s as glandular fever, but no infectious agent had been identified. The Henles made the link between a disease without a cause (infectious mononucleosis) and a virus (EBV) that had previously only been associated with Burkitt's lymphoma. Further work confirmed that EBV causes mononucleosis when it infects young adults but causes few symptoms when it infects children.

3

The Life of Epstein-Barr Virus

A HOME FOR EPSTEIN-BARR VIRUS: B CELLS

Epstein-Barr virus (EBV), as with all viruses, can take over the cell's chemical machinery and direct the cell to produce more viruses, a process called **virus replication**. A look at the structure of both the **host** cells and the virus will make the infection process easier to understand.

Once EBV gets inside the body through the lining of the nose and throat, it infects white blood cells called **B cells** (Figure 3.1). B cells are found in the blood circulation and in the **spleen** and **lymph nodes**. The B cells recognize disease-causing **pathogens** (path-oh-jens), such as viruses and bacteria, and kill them by making antibodies (this process is described in Chapter 4).

Human B cells are about 10 micrometers in diameter, about an eighth of the diameter of a human hair. A **plasma membrane** surrounds each B cell (Figure 3.2). The membrane is a very thin covering, like the "skin" of a soap bubble, and is made of **phospholipids** (a kind of fat). The membrane is solid, but proteins float on its surface as though it were liquid, like boats float on water. The plasma membrane and its proteins control what substances enter and leave the cell. Some B cell membrane proteins are **receptors** that bind pathogens; others are receptors for signaling molecules from other white blood cells. Still other membrane proteins allow the B cells to attach to the walls of blood vessels and enter the spleen and lymph nodes, where they produce antibodies.

Inside the plasma membrane, a gel-like substance, the **cytoplasm**, surrounds many small structures called **organelles**. Each organelle has its

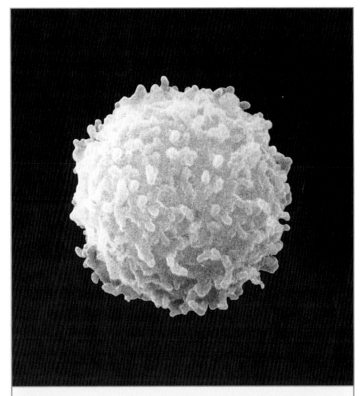

Figure 3.1 Once EBV enters the body, it infects a special class of white blood cells known as B cells (an electron micrograph of a single B cell is shown here). B cells normally recognize foreign organisms and produce antibodies against those organisms.

own membrane, and each contains enzymes. **Enzymes** are the protein catalysts that perform all the chemical reactions the B cell needs to survive and make antibodies. **Lysosomes** contain digestive enzymes that break large molecules into their building blocks that can then be used to make other molecules the cell needs. **Mitochondria** are responsible for converting energy from the sugars, proteins, and fats we eat into an energy storage molecule called **ATP**. This energy can later be used by the B cell to make enzymes or antibody proteins. The **Golgi complex**

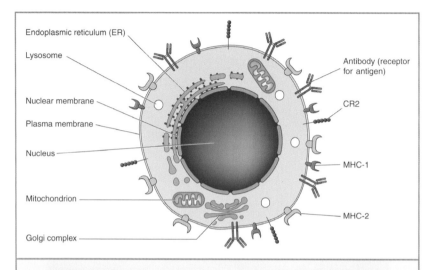

Endoplasmic reticulum (ER)

Lysosome

Antibody (receptor for antigen)

Nuclear membrane

CR2

Plasma membrane

Nucleus

MHC-1

Mitochondrion

MHC-2

Golgi complex

Figure 3.2 The B lymphocyte is surrounded by a plasma membrane containing protein receptors that the B cell uses to bind antigen and communicate with T cells. CR2 molecules allow EBV to infect B cells. New EBV is produced in the B cell nucleus. (The major histocompatability complex (MHC) is a set of genes with immunological and nonimmunological functions.)

forms the transport system of the cell, moving enzymes to the location where they are needed or exporting antibodies from the cell in membrane-bound **vesicles** (bubbles).

Deep inside the cell is the **nucleus**. The nuclear membrane surrounds the double helix DNA, which has all the genetic information the B cell needs to produce the thousands of enzymes and proteins that form its structure and regulate its function. When a particular protein is needed, the cell copies the DNA instructions for making that protein into messenger RNA. The messenger RNA leaves the nucleus and binds to **ribosomes**, where it is translated (copied) into the protein.

POISON WRAPPED IN A PROTEIN

Sir Peter Medawar, winner of the 1960 Nobel Prize in Physiology or Medicine, said "A virus is a piece of bad news wrapped

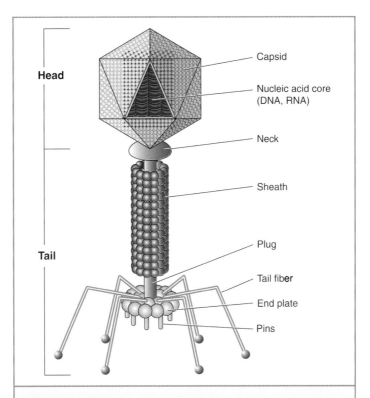

Figure 3.3 A virus is not considered a cell, because it cannot replicate on its own. It must "hijack" the cellular machinery of another cell to reproduce. Viruses are much smaller than even the smallest cell. They are composed of DNA or RNA wrapped in a protein coat called the capsid. They also usually contain a mechanism, such as spikes or pins, which allows them to attach to their target host cell. The general structure of a virus that infects bacteria is shown here.

in a protein." [1] Viruses (Figure 3.3) are much smaller and simpler than B cells. They are not even living cells, because they cannot perform the chemical reactions needed to use energy and produce more viruses. Viruses depend on the cells they infect, their host cells, to perform these processes.

The simplest viruses, which include the rhinovirus (cold virus), poliovirus, and hepatitis A virus, are only

24 to 30 nanometers (nm) in diameter. Five hundred rhino-viruses could fit across the diameter of a B cell. Their genetic information is contained in a single strand of RNA, much like messenger RNA, which is surrounded by a protein coat called a **capsid**. The capsid is an **icosahedron** with 20 identical triangular-shaped sides. The capsid and genetic material together are called the **nucleocapsid**. Rhinovirus RNA carries enough information for 11 proteins. Only four of these proteins are present in the virus; the others are required inside the host cell for virus replication and assembly.

Poxviruses, such as smallpox virus, are the largest viruses. They are brick-shaped and about 300 nm long. Their double-stranded DNA encodes more than 100 genes. The pox virus capsid is dumbbell-shaped and is surrounded by a lipid **envelope**. The envelope is similar to the host cell plasma membrane, but contains virus proteins. In addition to rhinoviruses and poxviruses, there are other viruses with double-stranded RNA or single-stranded DNA as genetic material and with helical as well as icosahedral capsids.

EBV is one of the larger viruses, 120 to 130 nm in diameter (Figure 3.4). Its capsid, composed of six different proteins, is icosahedral and surrounds a double-stranded DNA chromo-some, encoding more than 100 genes. The EBV nucleocapsid is surrounded by a group of 15 to 20 proteins called the **tegument**. A lipid envelope that was formerly part of the host cell plasma membrane surrounds the tegument. Protein **spikes** sticking out of the envelope allow the virus to bind to and infect host cells. Altogether, more than 30 proteins are part of the EBV structure, and many more virus proteins function inside the host cell.

Think of two soap bubbles that collide with one another and fuse to become one bubble. When an EBV particle enters the nose or throat, EBV collides with the epithelial cells that line the respiratory tract (Figure 3.5). EBV spike protein binds to an epithelial cell plasma membrane protein called CR2.

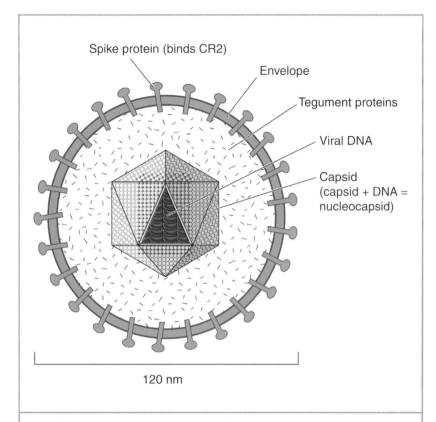

Figure 3.4 EBV is an enveloped DNA virus. Its double-stranded DNA genome is surrounded by an icosahedral (20-sided) capsid. Its envelope was part of the host cell nuclear membrane. Spike protein allows EBV to bind to and infect B cells and epithelial cells. The Epstein-Barr virus is illustrated here.

CR2 is present on the plasma membrane of epithelial cells in the nose and throat and on B cells.

Binding of the spike protein and CR2 brings the virus envelope and the host cell membrane into close contact. The EBV envelope fuses with the plasma membrane of the host cell just like the soap bubbles fused. The virus nucleocapsid is now in the cytoplasm of the host cell. After the nucleocapsid moves to the host cell nucleus, the virus DNA passes into the nucleus

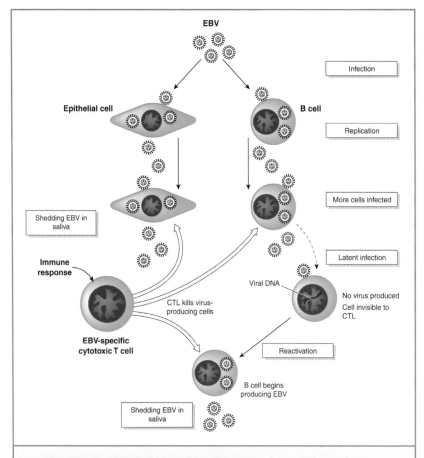

EBV

Infection

Epithelial cell

B cell

Replication

More cells infected

Shedding EBV in saliva

Latent infection

Immune response

Viral DNA

CTL kills virus-producing cells

No virus produced
Cell invisible to CTL

EBV-specific cytotoxic T cell

Reactivation

B cell begins producing EBV

Shedding EBV in saliva

Figure 3.5 **EBV infects both epithelial cells and B cells. Infected cells producing EBV are killed by cytotoxic T cells (CTL), but infected cells not producing EBV (latent infection) escape cell death and can later produce more EBV. EBV is shed in the saliva to infect new hosts.**

through a pore in the nuclear membrane to begin the process of virus replication.

From the virus DNA, messenger RNAs are made for proteins called early antigens that allow the virus to control chemical reactions in the host cell. The host cell messenger RNA is destroyed. Instead of making its own proteins, the cell begins to make virus proteins that alter the host cell enzymes to make thousands of copies of EBV DNA and EBV capsid, tegument, and spike proteins. The spike proteins are inserted into the host cell nuclear membrane, crowding out its normal proteins where the spike proteins are inserted. New EBV capsids assemble in the host cell nucleus and are filled with EBV DNA. As each nucleocapsid moves toward the nuclear membrane, it becomes surrounded with tegument proteins. Finally, the virus pushes the nuclear membrane outward in a process called **budding** until the membrane completely surrounds the nucleocapsid, forming the virus envelope. The new virus particles travel in vesicles and are expelled from the cell by fusion of the vesicle membrane with the plasma membrane. Thousands of virus particles may bud from a cell before it dies. EBV buds from the body side as well as the throat side of the epithelial cells. Some virus particles travel in the tissue fluid into the lymph nodes, tonsils, and salivary glands. In the lymph nodes and tonsils, EBV finds B cells to infect.

EBV proteins cause infected B cells to divide because during cell division, the B cells make proteins that help replicate the virus. As the B cells divide, they produce the antibody that helps diagnose mononucleosis. Normally, B cells live for a short time and then undergo **apoptosis**, programmed cell death. During programmed cell death, the DNA is cut into pieces and the cell disintegrates. Apoptosis occurs in many different cell types. In B cells that are produced to fight a particular pathogen, apoptosis removes those cells when they are no longer needed. In this way, the body guards itself against a prolonged immune response that can be damaging. EBV proteins block apoptosis in infected B cells so the cells survive to continue producing viruses.

Herpesviruses, including EBV, are able to establish **latent infection** in some cells. In latent infection, the EBV DNA is present in the B cell nucleus as a separate piece of DNA called an **episome**. The episome is attached to the host cell DNA at one point by a virus protein called Epstein-Barr nuclear antigen (EBNA-1), so that the EBV DNA is copied when the host cell DNA is copied. When the host B cell divides, one copy of the episome goes into each new cell. Latently infected B cells do not produce new viruses, so they do not look infected to the immune system. If the B cell containing a latent EBV is stimulated by an antigen to produce an antibody, it can also begin producing new EBV particles. This process is called **reactivation** and is responsible for virus shedding in the saliva of an infected but asymptomatic person months or years after they originally became infected.

NAMING VIRUSES

As viruses were discovered, their discoverers named them. Groups of viruses were often named for their physical properties: Parvoviruses are small viruses (parvo is the Latin word for small). Picornaviruses are small (pico) viruses that have RNA genes. Hepadna viruses are DNA-containing viruses that infect the liver and cause hepatitis.

Most individual viruses were named for the disease they caused: polio, measles, mumps, rubella, and hepatitis (several different hepatitis viruses are now named hepatitis A through hepatitis G). EBV was named for its discoverers. Hantaviruses were named for the Hantaan Peninsula of Korea where the kidney disease they cause was first identified during the Korean War. The related hantavirus discovered in the American Southwest was unofficially called Four Corners virus because the first people who died from it came from the area where the corners of Arizona, New Mexico, Colorado, and Utah come together. It was then called *Canyon del Muerto* virus after a nearby location on the Navajo reservation. No people wanted this deadly virus named after their home, so it was finally named *Sin Nombre virus*, Spanish for "no name."

In rare cases, the virus DNA integrates into (becomes part of) the B cell DNA. Sometimes **viral integration** causes the B cell to divide uncontrollably and become a cancer cell. Cancer formation induced by EBV is rare in the United States, but is more common in parts of Africa and Asia where other factors called cocarcinogens are present. Cancer associated with EBV infection is discussed in Chapter 9.

THE HERPESVIRUS FAMILY

Epstein-Barr virus is a member of the herpesvirus family of DNA viruses. Herpesviruses can infect all

The issue of virus naming became important with the discovery of the virus that causes AIDS. Luc Montagnier's group at the Pasteur Institute in Paris named it LAV (lymphadenopathy-associated virus) because it was found in the swollen lymph nodes of people with AIDS. At the National Institutes of Health in Washington, D.C., a group led by Robert Gallo isolated the same virus and called it HTLV-III for human T cell leukemia because it resembled the viruses isolated from people with T cell leukemia (a cancer of the T cells). It is now believed that Gallo's tissue cultures became infected with a virus that had been sent from Montagnier's lab, since LAV and HTLV-III were identical. An international committee settled the dispute in 1986 by recommending that the virus be named human immunodeficiency virus (HIV). They suggested that viruses should be named according to the species they infect and the disease they cause, for example tobacco mosaic virus or human herpesvirus-4. However, since 1999, the spread of West Nile virus across the United States still reflects the geographic origins of the virus rather than the human and bird encephalitis (brain inflammation) it causes.

vertebrates and oysters. These viruses have adapted themselves to the immune system and have developed several strategies for avoiding elimination by it. Eight distinct herpesviruses have been identified in humans. Each causes a different disease. EBV is sometimes called human herpesvirus-4, or HHV-4.

Three of the herpesviruses can infect nervous tissue: herpes simplex virus I (**HSV**-I), herpes simplex virus II (HSV-II), and varicella-zoster virus (**VZV**). HSV-I usually causes cold sores around the mouth, and HSV-II causes genital herpes, although each can infect the other's territory. They enter the body through the mucous membranes of the mouth or genital tract and cause sores at the site of infection. The immune system kills most of the virus particles, but a few can hide in nerve cells and cause recurrent infections when immunity drops or when activated by ultraviolet light. The tingling felt before a cold sore erupts is the HSV-I traveling down the nerve to reinfect skin cells on the face. VZV causes the skin rash of chicken pox. VZV can also hide in nerve cells and reappear to cause the very painful rash called shingles.

Five other herpesviruses infect cells of the immune system. They are EBV, cytomegalovirus (**CMV**), and human herpesviruses HHV-6, HHV-7, and HHV-8.

EBV causes infectious mononucleosis and, in rare cases, Burkitt's lymphoma or nasopharyngeal carcinoma. CMV also causes a form of mononucleosis and can infect the nervous system of babies before birth. HHV-6 (also called roseola virus) and HHV-7 cause mild childhood infections. HHV-8 has been found in Kaposi's sarcoma, a skin tumor seen in some people with AIDS.

B virus is a herpesvirus that infects old-world primates, for example rhesus and cynomolgus monkeys. In its primate hosts, B virus resembles HSV-1 and causes generally mild infections of the skin, mouth, eyes, and genital tract. In humans who contract it from primate bites or saliva or from working with monkey cell cultures, B virus causes a life-threatening nervous system infection.

4

Immune System Response to Epstein-Barr Virus

The job of the immune system is to recognize and eliminate **pathogens**, infectious agents that cause disease. The immune system is composed of the white blood cells (also called **leukocytes**, Figure 4.1) and collections of leukocytes in several organs: the lymph nodes, spleen, tonsils, and appendix. Leukocytes are produced in the bone marrow along with **erythrocytes** (red blood cells, or RBCs). Figure 4.2 shows the location of some of the organs of the immune system.

The immune system is designed to be able to tell the difference between "self" antigens and "nonself," or foreign, antigens. **Antigens** are the chemical parts of human and pathogen cells, such as proteins and sugars, that can be recognized by the immune system. The presence of foreign antigens signals the immune system to become active and eliminate the pathogen.

The body's immune response is a key part of infectious mononucleosis. One reason is because Epstein-Barr virus (EBV) infects B cells, which participate in the body's defenses against infectious disease. Also, the illness is probably more severe in young adults as compared to children because of a stronger immune response in young adults against the virus. Finally, EBV has adapted to the immune system and alters it so that the virus can remain in the body indefinitely.

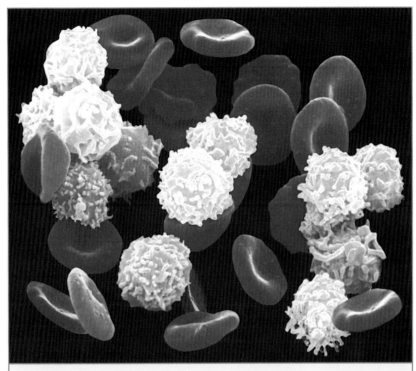

Figure 4.1 Blood is composed of red and white blood cells (both are shown in this electron micrograph). The white blood cells are part of the immune system and help to fight off pathogens.

INITIAL RESPONSE: INFLAMMATION

Our skin is one of our key defenses against disease. Viruses cannot penetrate or infect the thickened dead cells that cover most of the outside of our bodies. The mucous membranes of our noses and mouths, digestive, urinary, and genital tracts, and around our eyes are weak points in the barrier. Once EBV infects the epithelial cells of the mouth, it has a route into the body, and the immune system goes to work.

When one person kisses another, some viruses in the saliva of one person use their spike proteins to bind to and infect the epithelial cells of the other person's mouth. Other

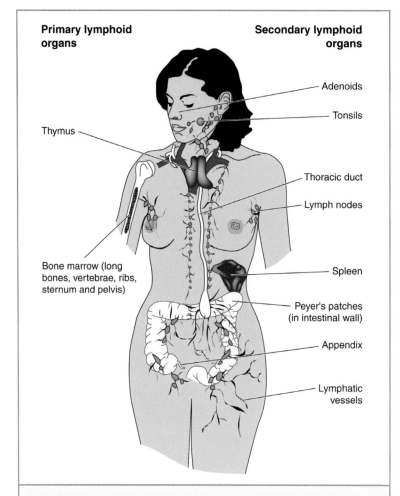

Primary lymphoid organs

Secondary lymphoid organs

Adenoids

Tonsils

Thymus

Thoracic duct

Lymph nodes

Bone marrow (long bones, vertebrae, ribs, sternum and pelvis)

Spleen

Peyer's patches (in intestinal wall)

Appendix

Lymphatic vessels

Figure 4.2 The immune system consists of white blood cells, which are created and stored in several organs. The primary organs of the immune system include the thymus and the bone marrow. The secondary organs include the tonsils, the spleen, the lymph nodes, and the appendix.

EBV particles are washed into the person's throat and infect the epithelial cells there. Damage to the cells of the throat and the body's immune response to the infection cause the initial sore throat and fatigue. However, many other events are happening as the virus replicates and spreads through the body.

As the virus replicates in the epithelial cells of the throat, new viruses bud from the cells on the inside surface, toward the deeper tissues of the mouth and throat. More cells become infected, and some cells begin to die because all their energy is used to make new EBV particles. The dead cells disintegrate, and their contents, as well as pieces of unfinished viruses, are released into the tissues around them. Cell damage initiates inflammation, the initial immune response that begins within minutes and continues throughout the active virus infection.

Macrophages, whose name means "big eaters," live in all body tissues and are the first cells to detect trouble. Macrophages are **phagocytes** (FAG-oh-sites), "eating cells," whose primary job is to engulf and destroy dead cells and pathogens that have entered the body through the mucous membranes or after injury to the skin.

Macrophage membranes are covered with receptor proteins that bind molecules from the dead cells and signal the macrophages that there is trouble. The macrophages put out long fingers of cytoplasm to surround the pieces of dead cells and take them inside the macrophage in membrane-covered bubbles called phagosomes. The macrophage then moves lysosomes full of digestive enzymes toward and into the phagosomes, so that the dead cells and any pathogens inside them are digested into small molecules. This process of binding, engulfing, and destroying pathogens and dead cells is called **phagocytosis** (fag-oh-sy-TOE-sis) (Figure 4.3).

The macrophages also respond by producing and secreting **cytokines**, protein signals that travel through the tissues and into the bloodstream. Some of these cytokines signal nearby macrophages that there is danger, and the macrophages crawl through the tissues toward the site of infection. Other cytokines signal cells lining nearby blood vessels to make new membrane proteins that alert passing white blood cells that an

Figure 4.3 Macrophages engulf foreign particles through the process of phagocytosis, illustrated here. The macrophage stretches out arm-like projections that surround the particle, drawing it into the cell. The macrophage then secretes special enzymes that break down the foreign particle.

infection is occurring. Blood macrophages and **neutrophils** (NEWT-row-fills), another kind of phagocyte, follow the cytokine trail toward the infection site. They stick to and crawl between the cells of the blood vessels to enter the tissues, where they engulf and destroy dead cells and virus pieces. In response to macrophage cytokines, the blood vessels become leaky, allowing the fluid part of the blood to enter the tissues.

Cell damage activates another group of blood proteins called complement. When complement proteins are activated, some of them bind to blood vessel walls and make the vessels leaky so more complement proteins can enter the infection site. Other complement proteins attract neutrophils and macrophages to the site of infection. Still others coat the pathogen and then bind to complement receptors on macrophages and neutrophils, so the pathogens are more efficiently engulfed and destroyed. The CR2 protein, the epithelial cell plasma membrane protein that EBV uses to infect B cells and epithelial cells, is one of these complement receptors.

Macrophages and neutrophils bind to pieces of dead cells, but they cannot do anything about infected cells that are still healthy enough to continue producing thousands of viruses to spread the infection to more and more of the infected person's throat cells. Virus infection induces cells to produce proteins called **interferons** because they interfere with virus replication. Interferon alpha and interferon beta secreted from infected cells bind to nearby cells and prevent them from manufacturing virus proteins.

Some of the virus proteins made inside infected cells are cut into small pieces (**peptides**) and combined with a cell protein called **MHC-1**. MHC proteins are the tissue-typing proteins that must be matched in a transplant. Their job in infected cells is to carry virus peptides to the plasma membrane. There the peptides tell specialized white blood cells that the epithelial cell is infected. The white blood cells then kill the infected cell to stop virus production. Every cell in the body except red blood cells has MHC-1 and can use it to signal when a virus has infected the cell. Because red blood cells do not have a nucleus and do not synthesize proteins, viruses do not infect them.

The first cells to recognize virus peptides on an infected cell's MHC-1 are called **natural killer** (NK) cells. NK cells cannot tell what kind of virus is infecting the cell, only that the MHC-1 has "foreign" peptides bound to it. The NK cells crawl through the infected tissues, and when they find a cell with foreign peptide on its MHC-1, they bind tightly to the infected cell and release little packets of killing enzymes. The killing enzymes enter the infected cell and kill it, halting virus replication in that cell. The NK cell then crawls away and looks for other infected cells to kill. The macrophage cytokines that make blood vessels leaky and attract more leukocytes to the infection site also stimulate NK cells to be more active killers of EBV-infected cells. As the NK cells kill more infected cells, the cell damage signals macrophages to produce still more cytokines.

The site of EBV infection becomes swollen with fluid and white blood cells, pressing on nerves and giving the infected person a sore throat. Increased blood flow to the area makes the throat red. This entire process is called **inflammation** and is the body's first response to infection. Cytokines have also traveled to the brain and signaled it to increase the body temperature, causing a fever. Fever allows the immune system to work better and slows the growth of some pathogens. Other cytokines make the infected person feel very tired, so that the person will rest and let the body use its energy to fight the infection.

As the throat tissues swell, macrophages and fluid drain into nearby clusters of tissues called lymph nodes, the "glands" of glandular fever. Lymph nodes are the location where the immune system will begin to produce antibodies and cytotoxic (cell-killing) **T cells** that will remove most of the EBV and relieve the person's symptoms. Lymph nodes are located all over the body to filter out pathogens and activate B and T cells. Tonsils are similar lymphoid organs in the throat. The tonsils and lymph nodes are also the places where EBV can find another cell to infect: the B cell. Viruses also travel to the salivary glands where they can be shed into the saliva.

SPECIFIC RESPONSE: CYTOTOXIC T CELLS

Macrophages and neutrophils respond to common danger signals and enter the infection site to remove dead cells and pieces of EBV. For the body to find and remove EBV from infected cells, white blood cells called T cells and B cells must become involved. T and B cells are **lymphocytes**. As lymphocytes are produced, their DNA is altered so that each cell makes membrane receptors that recognize one specific foreign antigen. During this process, other lymphocytes are also made that recognize "self" antigens, but those lymphocytes are killed before they can damage the body. When EBV enters a person's body, T and B cells that recognize EBV antigens will be stimulated to **proliferate** (undergo cell division) to produce many new T and B cells. The T and B cells will also **differentiate** (change their activities) to eliminate infected cells and virus particles. **Memory cells** that can recognize EBV and respond more quickly in the future will also be made. This is called the adaptive immune response and takes several days to several weeks to control the infection. The adaptive immune response works with inflammation, which continues as long as viruses are being produced by infected cells.

T cells resemble NK cells because they can only detect antigen that is "presented" on MHC proteins. There are two kinds of T cells, **cytotoxic T cells** and **helper T cells**. Cytotoxic T cells recognize virus peptides presented by infected cells on MHC-1. Helper T cells recognize virus peptides presented on MHC-2 by specialized antigen-presenting cells. Both kinds of

T cells circulate in the blood and collect in the lymph nodes, spleen, and tonsils.

In addition to the epithelial cells and the macrophages in the tissues of the infected person's throat are star-shaped cells called dendritic cells (the long arms of the stars are called dendrites). Dendritic cells, like epithelial cells and B cells, have the CR2 protein on their membranes that allows EBV to infect them. EBV-infected dendritic cells go to the nearby lymph nodes, which are full of resting T and B cells, waiting for their specific antigen to appear. As the dendritic cells crawl through the lymph nodes, resting cytotoxic T cells with membrane receptors for EBV peptides bind the peptide-MHC-1 complexes on the surface of the dendritic cells. The dendritic cells and cytotoxic T cells exchange chemical signals. The cytotoxic T cells respond to the signals by proliferating into thousands of identical cytotoxic T cells, all with receptor proteins that recognize EBV peptides on MHC-1. The new killer cells also become larger and produce packets of killing enzymes in their cytoplasm.

When cytotoxic T cells are fully active, many leave the lymph nodes and enter the blood. A blood test will show high numbers of mononuclear cells because cytotoxic T cells travel in the blood to the infected person's throat. When the cytotoxic T cells find the blood vessel with proteins marking the site of infection, the cytotoxic T cells crawl out of the blood vessel and into the throat's epithelial tissue. Whenever a cytotoxic T cell finds an infected cell with MHC-1 containing virus peptide, the T cell binds tightly to the infected cell and secretes its packets of enzymes to kill the infected cell (Figure 4.4). As the infected cell dies, macrophages and neutrophils engulf and destroy the cell and all the virus pieces it contains. Uninfected cells do not have virus peptides on their MHC-1, so the cytotoxic T cells do not harm them. As infection shifts to the B cells, cytotoxic T cells find and kill infected B cells in the blood and lymph nodes.

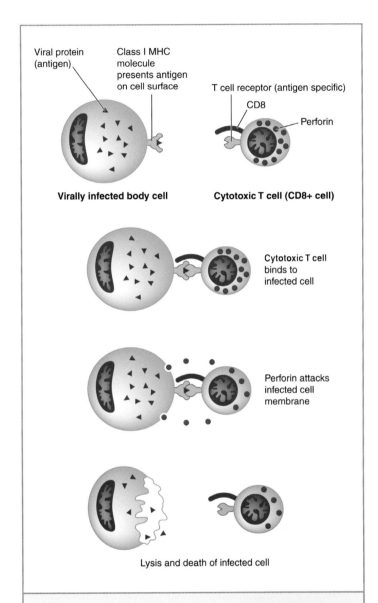

Figure 4.4 Infected cells display small pieces of EBV antigens on their Class I MHC (MHC-I). Cytotoxic T cells that bind EBV antigens on Class I MHC release perforin, which attacks the infected cell. The perforin eats holes in the infected cell membrane through which enzymes enter to kill the infected cell.

As the number of infected cells decreases, the amount of inflammation in the area also decreases, and the infected person's throat will no longer feel sore. The fever will drop, and the person will slowly get his or her energy back.

SPECIFIC RESPONSE: ANTIBODY PRODUCTION

As infected cells are killed and virus proteins are released, the phagocytes are responsible for engulfing those proteins and destroying them. Phagocytes have receptors that allow them to bind bacteria, but they are much less efficient at binding viruses and virus proteins. To aid the phagocytes, B cells must make antibody proteins.

Antibodies are Y-shaped proteins that can bind antigen with each arm of the Y (Figure 4.5). As B cells are made in the bone marrow, B cell DNA rearranges so that each new B cell makes a different antibody protein able to bind a different antigen. The new B cell uses some of this antibody as a membrane receptor for antigen. Like T cells, new resting B cells circulate in the blood and collect in the lymph nodes, tonsils, and spleen where they wait for their specific antigen to appear.

Some of the EBV proteins released from the infected cells in the throat drain into the nearby lymph nodes and tonsils. Specific B cells that bind EBV to their antibody receptors take some of the EBV proteins into the cell and combine EBV peptides with MHC-2. They then put the peptide-MHC-2 complexes on their membranes, where nearby helper T cells can recognize them. The helper T cells and the B cells bind tightly together and exchange chemical signals. Both cell types proliferate into thousands of helper T cells and B cells, all specific for EBV (Figure 4.6). Cytokines from the helper T cells signal the B cells to secrete antibody molecules. The antibodies travel in the blood to the throat, where the blood vessels are leaky and the antibodies can enter the tissues.

The antibodies bind the EBV with the arms of the Y. The tail of the Y binds to specialized receptors on the macrophages

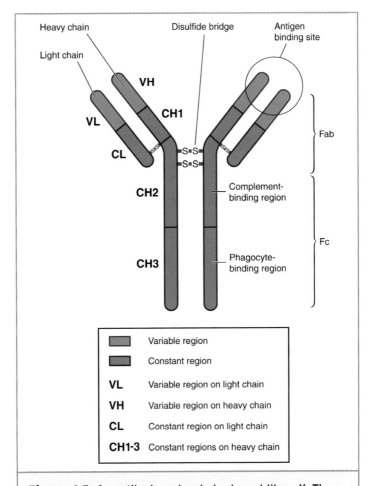

Heavy chain   Disulfide bridge   Antigen binding site

Light chain

VH

CH1

VL

CL

S•S
S•S

CH2   Complement-binding region

Fab

CH3   Phagocyte-binding region

Fc

	Variable region
	Constant region
VL	Variable region on light chain
VH	Variable region on heavy chain
CL	Constant region on light chain
CH1-3	Constant regions on heavy chain

Figure 4.5 An antibody molecule is shaped like a Y. The "stem" of the Y is the constant region and is the same for all antibodies. The "arms" are variable and differ depending upon the antigen for which the antibody is specific. EBV binds to the variable region of each "arm" of the Y. The "stem" of the Y binds to phagocytes to help them engulf EBV.

and neutrophils. These receptors allow the phagocytes to bind tightly to the virus particles, engulf, and kill them. Macrophages and neutrophils remove viruses much more efficiently in the presence of antibodies. (Imagine that the antibody Ys

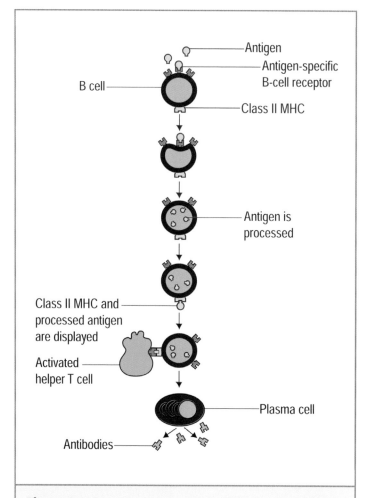

B cell

Antigen

Antigen-specific
B-cell receptor

Class II MHC

Antigen is
processed

Class II MHC and
processed antigen
are displayed

Activated
helper T cell

Plasma cell

Antibodies

Figure 4.6 Some B cells have antibody molecules that bind
EBV. The EBV is taken into the cell, cut into pieces, and
displayed on Class II MHC. Helper T cells recognize the
EBV-MHC II complex and signal the B cells to secrete
EBV-specific antibodies.

are "forks" that the macrophages and neutrophils use to pick
up viruses with their receptor "hands.") Antibody-coated
viruses activate more complement proteins, and the combina-
tion of antibody and complement proteins increases the ease

with which phagocytes engulf EBV. Antibodies coating the spike proteins on whole viruses prevent those viruses from using the spike proteins to infect new cells. This blocking process is caused **virus neutralization**.

Antibodies cannot cross the plasma membrane of infected cells, so they can only neutralize and promote the phagocytosis of viruses and virus proteins that have been released from host cells. For the host to stop the virus infection, it must use cytotoxic T cells to kill all the infected cells and release the viruses. Nevertheless, antibodies do speed the virus removal process.

MEMORY: IMMUNITY TO EBV

Immunity is the ability to resist disease. Sometimes we become immune after we have a disease. For example, children who have had chicken pox do not generally get chicken pox again. We also become immune after we have been vaccinated. Vaccines like measles, mumps, and rubella (MMR) expose us to weakened forms of viruses that cannot make us sick, but do signal specific T and B cells to divide and make memory cells. Memory cells resemble resting T and B cells, but they are more numerous and they become activated much faster to produce killer enzymes or antibodies. Once we have memory cells, we may become infected by a pathogen, but the pathogen is eliminated before we have any disease symptoms.

Infection with EBV results in the production of memory T and B cells specific for EBV. Memory cells circulate in the blood and congregate in the lymph nodes, spleen, and tonsils where they are ready to respond quickly if any more viruses are produced. EBV can remain in the body only by becoming a latent virus, one that stays in the cells without being replicated.

5

Signs and Symptoms

TYPICAL INFECTIOUS MONONUCLEOSIS

The week after Thanksgiving, Rob developed a low-grade fever, lost his appetite, had a headache, and was very tired, even in the morning. When the symptoms, especially the fatigue, persisted for two weeks, Rob decided to see his family physician. Blood test results showed a white blood cell count about twice the normal level, with increased numbers of lymphocytes and decreased numbers of neutrophils. Thirty percent of the lymphocytes looked unusual. The results of the blood test also showed the presence of two antibodies, one type that clumped sheep red blood cells and another type to an Epstein-Barr virus viral capsid antigen, **VCA**. Based on these results, Rob's physician diagnosed infectious mononucleosis. Rob's sore throat and fever disappeared after about three weeks, but he felt abnormally tired for several months after the infection.

Disease symptoms are changes in the body that the patient reports. **Disease signs** are changes in the body that the physician can see or measure. Rob's signs and symptoms are typical of infectious mononucleosis in a young adult. Fever lasting 10 to 14 days, an extremely sore throat for 3 to 5 days, enlarged tonsils and lymph nodes in the neck, and fatigue are experienced by almost everyone who has infectious mononucleosis. When these symptoms appear in someone in their mid-teens to mid-twenties, infectious mononucleosis is the likely cause. Someone with infectious mononucleosis might also complain of headache, loss of appetite, and muscle aches. The **incubation period** for the disease, which is the time between exposure to the virus and the time symptoms occur, may be as long as 4 to 6 weeks.

Clinical signs of the disease include an inflamed throat, swollen tonsils, and an enlarged spleen, which is in the upper left area of the abdomen. The spleen, as well as tonsils and lymph nodes, is enlarged because of the T and B cells multiplying there in response to EBV antigens. The key sign is the appearance of the blood smear under the microscope.

Blood tests usually confirm the diagnosis of infectious mononucleosis. As cytotoxic T cells enter the blood circulation to go to the site of infection, their numbers increase. Their appearance is different from the resting T cells that are usually in the blood, and they are classified as "atypical" or unusual lymphocytes (Figure 5.1). Antibodies to EBV as well as the **heterophile** antibodies to sheep red blood cells in the blood are a clear sign that the patient has mononucleosis. Because it infects the immune cells that produce antibodies, EBV causes antibody production to many different antigens, including sugars on the outside of red blood cells. Clumping of sheep red blood cells is a quick and inexpensive test for heterophile antibodies, which are not present in other infections. Someone with antibodies to EBV is called seropositive for EBV, meaning their blood serum (the liquid part) tests positive for EBV antibodies. Once people have been infected with EBV, they remain seropositive for the rest of their lives. People who have not been infected and do not have antibodies to EBV are called seronegative.

Babies are born with antibodies from their mothers that protect them from infectious disease. As they lose these antibodies during their first year of life, they become susceptible to EBV infection. Young children often have no symptoms when they become infected with EBV. Symptoms that do occur in young children are typical of many childhood diseases and often pass unnoticed. Sometimes children (and more rarely, adults) will have a skin rash (Figure 5.2) that does not itch and a mild fever. Their blood tests show a decrease in the numbers of neutrophils, but only half of them may have heterophile antibodies. Small

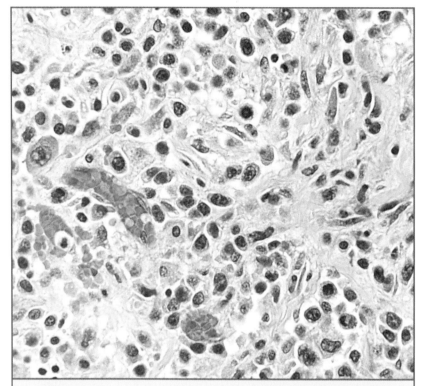

Figure 5.1 This image shows a blood smear of a person with atypical lymphocytes (notice the red, abnormally shaped cells in the smear).

children also occasionally get pneumonia from EBV. Experts believe that the lack of symptoms in younger children is because of their less mature immune systems.

Among college-age men and women, only one in three shows no symptoms when infected with EBV. The number of people becoming infected without symptoms has been estimated to be one in ten among military recruits.

RARE COMPLICATIONS

Nearly everyone who gets infectious mononucleosis recovers in less than two months. Although they carry the virus in a few of

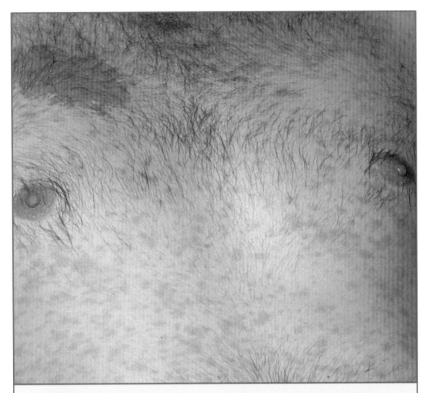

Figure 5.2 Sometimes EBV will cause a red skin rash, as seen in this photo. Other symptoms include fever, swollen glands, sore throat, and fatigue.

their B cells and can periodically shed it in their saliva for life, they usually do not become ill with mononucleosis again.

The spleen is an organ in the abdomen that has two functions. Like the lymph nodes, the spleen is a collection of T and B lymphocytes, macrophages, and dendritic cells. The spleen filters pathogens and their antigens from the blood and is a site of T and B cell activation and antibody synthesis. The spleen is also the place where old red blood cells are removed from the blood and destroyed. In mononucleosis, the spleen becomes swollen with both red and white blood cells. Rarely, it can rupture, particularly after a blow to the abdomen. A ruptured spleen is a life-threatening event, because massive bleeding occurs in the abdomen. Someone with a ruptured spleen experiences pain in the upper left part of the abdomen and becomes pale and sweaty from shock. Immediate emergency surgery is required to remove the spleen and stop the bleeding.

Other very rare complications include tonsils so swollen

CAN A PERSON SURVIVE WITHOUT A SPLEEN?

The spleen is the largest lymphoid organ in the body. One of the spleen's main functions, as part of the immune response, is to filter the blood of any pathogens that may be present. Blood is normally **sterile**, free of all bacteria and viruses. When bacteria enter the bloodstream or even grow there, they can quickly spread throughout the body and cause life-threatening infections.

The spleen also shares the liver's function of removing and destroying old red blood cells. As red blood cells age, enzymes in the blood remove sugars from their membrane proteins, exposing different sugars underneath. Phagocytic cells, called Kupffer cells, that line the liver blood vessels bind to those exposed sugars. The Kupffer cells then engulf and destroy the red blood cells. Iron is removed from the hemoglobin protein and recycled into new red blood cells. The hemoglobin is broken down and removed from the body in the intestines, where it makes solid waste brown.

Babies born without a spleen begin to have serious bacterial infections during their first year of life. They are especially susceptible to *Streptococcus pneumoniae* (STREP-toe-cock-us new-MOAN-ee-ay) and *Haemophilus influenzae* (he-MOFF-a-lus in-flu-en-zay). These bacteria cause ear infections and meningitis (infection of the brain and spinal cord coverings) in young children. The bacteria that they interfere with breathing. Tonsils are similar to lymph nodes, but 80% of their cells are B cells. When EBV infects some of those B cells and induces them to divide, the tonsils swell with the increased numbers of B cells. If the tonsils are so swollen that they block the throat, they must be removed.

are surrounded by sugar coatings, called capsules, which make it difficult for phagocytes to engulf them.

Older people who have their spleens removed have usually already made antibodies against *Streptococcus pneumoniae* and *Haemophilus influenzae*. When the bacteria enter the blood, antibodies coat them and the bacteria can then be removed and killed by the Kupffer cells in the liver. People with antibodies to *Streptococcus pneumoniae* and *Haemophilus influenzae* are still at increased risk of infection when they have dental work, as bacteria can easily enter the blood through the gums. If the person has an artificial joint or heart valve, they are at even higher risk because these are sites to which bacteria can adhere and begin multiplying. All people with artificial joints or heart valves must take antibiotics before and after visiting the dentist to kill any bacteria that have entered their bodies.

Babies are now routinely vaccinated against *Haemophilus influenzae* B with the HiB vaccine. The vaccine does not contain whole bacteria, but contains capsule antigen that induces the immune system to make antibodies to the capsules. Vaccinated children can easily remove blood *Haemophilus influenzae* in the liver. If a baby is found not to have a spleen or if a young child must have the spleen removed for some reason, he or she can also be vaccinated against the capsule of *Streptococcus pneumoniae*. Once the children have antibodies, their infection risk becomes the same as the adult risk of infection.

EBV infection can cause reduced levels of red blood cells (**anemia**), resulting in fatigue and shortness of breath. Numbers of platelets, the blood cells important for clotting, may decrease in the blood as increased bleeding or bruising from minor injuries occurs. Numbers of red blood cells (RBCs) and platelets also decrease if some of the heterophile antibodies damage them so that they are removed by the spleen or liver **Kupffer cells**.

GUILLAIN-BARRÉ SYNDROME

Guillain-Barré (ghee-yan bah-ray) syndrome is caused by the immune system attacking the peripheral nervous system. It usually begins with tingling and weakness in the legs, spreading to the arms and upper body. In severe cases of Guillain-Barré syndrome, the patient may become almost totally paralyzed and may need a ventilator to assist with breathing. Most people who develop Guillain-Barré syndrome recover fully.

Guillain-Barré syndrome is very rare. A virus infection can trigger Guillain-Barré syndrome; very occasionally vaccination or surgery seems to be the cause. It may come on suddenly or over the course of several weeks. Recovery can take from a few weeks to as long as a few years.

There is no specific treatment for Guillain-Barré syndrome, but several treatments can lessen its severity and speed the recovery of the affected person. One treatment is **plasmapherisis** (plasma-fur-EE-sis), a procedure that removes blood from the body and separates the cells from the **plasma** (the liquid part of blood). The cells are returned to the body, but the plasma is discarded. This treatment removes any plasma particles (including viruses) that might be causing the disease. The other treatment is intravenous administration of pooled antibody molecules (IVIG) from healthy blood donors. The IVIG contains antibodies specific for many common pathogens and can help macrophages and neutrophils remove the virus from the body.

EBV infection can cause hepatitis, an inflammation of the liver. Although liver enzyme levels increase in the blood of 80 to 90% of people who have mononucleosis, serious damage to the liver is uncommon. Occasionally liver damage results in **jaundice** (JAWN-dis), a yellowing of the skin. EBV may also cause inflammation of the heart.

Viruses, including EBV, can affect the central nervous system and cause paralysis and **meningitis**. Bell's palsy is facial paralysis associated with virus infections. Usually the face droops on one side. Most people with Bell's palsy recover fully. Guillain-Barré syndrome is another neurological disease that can follow virus infection. Meningitis is inflammation of the meninges, the membranes surrounding the brain and spinal cord. Symptoms of meningitis include fever and sleepiness.

6

EBV Transmission and Latent Infection

TRANSMISSION

EBV is a very fragile virus, and cannot survive long outside the human body. When an infected person touches his or her mouth and then the phone, the virus quickly dries out and is no longer infectious even if another person touches the phone and then his or her own nose or mouth. A person can only be infected by direct contact with the saliva of someone who has the virus. Infection can occur by kissing someone on the mouth who has EBV in his or her saliva or by sharing a straw or drinking vessel or eating utensil with that person.

Once people have been infected with EBV, the virus can be present in their saliva even after they no longer have symptoms. EBV is found in the saliva of 12 to 25% of healthy seropositive adults (those with antibodies to EBV). It is also present in the saliva of half of HIV-infected people and kidney transplant patients, and up to 100% of people who have the symptoms of mononucleosis. EBV is not found in the saliva of people who are seronegative for EBV (have never been infected).

Because it is transmitted only by direct contact, mononucleosis is not a particularly **contagious** disease. Family members and college roommates of people with mononucleosis are not likely to get the disease unless they kiss or share utensils with the infected person.

In unusual cases, EBV can be spread by blood transfusion, open heart surgery, or bone marrow transplantation. Because almost all people have been infected by the time they are adults, donated blood and bone marrow are not tested for the presence of EBV or antibody to EBV.

EBV infection occurs throughout the world. About 90 to 95% of adults worldwide are seropositive for EBV. In countries with lower standards of hygiene, most people are infected in childhood, and fewer have the classic symptoms of mononucleosis. In developed countries where the standards of hygiene are higher, about half of the people contract mononucleosis as children, and the others become infected when they are between 15 and 24 years old. Both men and women get EBV, but females become infected an average of two years younger than males.

Unlike colds and the flu, EBV does not occur more often during certain seasons of the year. **Epidemics**, in which large numbers of people become infected at the same time, are not seen with mononucleosis. Infectious mononucleosis is an **endemic** disease, always present in low numbers of people.

Students in college and the military experience the most illness from infectious mononucleosis. It is estimated that 12% of college students who were seronegative become seropositive each year. This percentage is probably a low estimate because some students will have no symptoms when they become infected. Mononucleosis is seen in these groups because they are coming in contact with new people, the stresses of college and military training may make them more susceptible to disease, and they are less likely to have asymptomatic infections because of their age.

LATENT INFECTION

As we saw in Chapter 3, B cells can bind EBV and make antibodies that coat the viruses. Coated viruses cannot infect new cells and are easier for the macrophages and neutrophils to engulf and kill. Natural killer (NK) cells and cytotoxic T cells recognize virus peptides on infected cell plasma membrane

MHC-1 and kill the host cell, releasing virus to be destroyed by the phagocytes. EBV has several ways in which it avoids recognition and destruction so that it can persist in the host and spread to new hosts.

Latent infection of B cells allows EBV to hide in the body undetected by the immune system (Figure 6.1). In latent infection, the virus DNA is present in the B cell nucleus, but no new viruses are being produced. Virus particles cannot be detected using tissue culture or polymerase chain reaction (see Chapter 7). Antibodies continue to be made by memory B cells, but the antibodies have no virus to bind. EBV DNA is present in B cells of half of the healthy children who have antibodies to EBV, so latent infection is very common.

EBV makes a few proteins during latent infection that keep the virus from being removed from the cell and prevent the B cell from dying of apoptosis. EBNA-1 (Epstein-Barr nuclear antigen, a virus protein), attaches the virus DNA to the host cell DNA, so they are replicated and distributed together during cell division. EBNA-1 has another function that protects the virus from cytotoxic T and NK cells. EBNA-1 blocks the cell from cutting virus proteins into peptides that can be combined with MHC-1. If no virus peptides are present on MHC-1, the infected B cells appear uninfected to the killer cells and are not destroyed.

INHIBITING THE IMMUNE RESPONSE

Cytokines are powerful molecules that are made by leukocytes and signal other cells to make an immune response. The immune system also makes suppressor cytokines that inhibit immune responses (Figure 6.2). Suppressor cytokines are important in preventing immune responses from accidentally destroying healthy cells. Immune responses against healthy tissue occur in

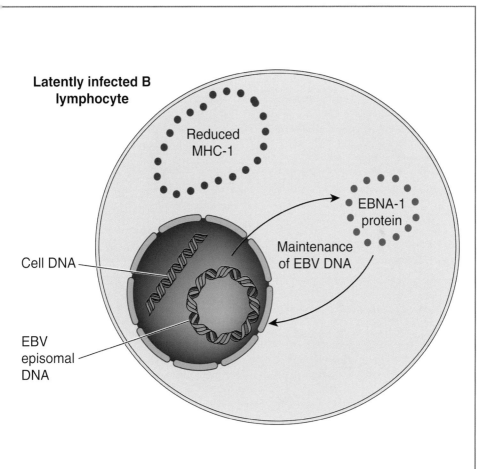

Latently infected B lymphocyte

Reduced MHC-1

EBNA-1 protein

Cell DNA

Maintenance of EBV DNA

EBV episomal DNA

Figure 6.1 EBV DNA is present in the latently infected B cell nucleus as a separate circular molecule (episome), as illustrated in this diagram. The EBV episome is much smaller than the host chromosomes. Episomal genes encode EBV proteins that keep the B cell from dying or losing the EBV DNA.

autoimmune diseases, such as multiple sclerosis and type-1 diabetes.

EBV has a gene for a virus protein that resembles a suppressor cytokine, interleukin-10 (IL-10). The virus protein

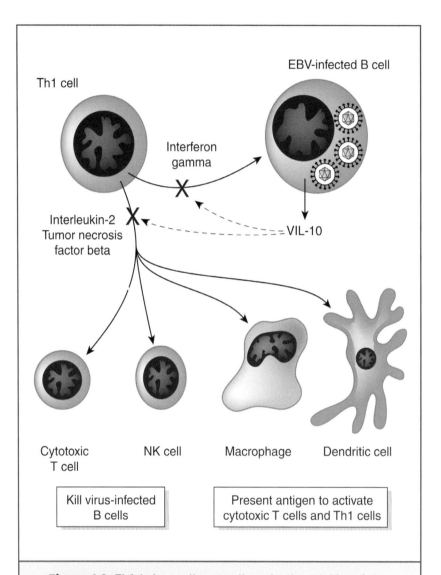

Figure 6.2 Th1 helper cells normally make the cytokines inter-
leukin-2 and tumor necrosis factor beta that help cytotoxic T
cells and NK cells kill EBV-infected B cells. The process is
illustrated in this diagram. Interferon gamma from Th1 cells
blocks EBV production in infected B cells. EBV protein vIL-10
blocks Th1 cytokine production and helps infected B cells
make more EBV.

is called vIL-10. EBV vIL-10 suppresses or inactivates Th1 cells, helper T cells that usually help activate cytotoxic T cells and NK cells. Th1 cells make interleukin-2 and tumor necrosis factor beta, cytokines that stimulate NK and cytotoxic T cells to kill virus-infected cells. The same cytokines stimulate macrophages and dendritic cells to make more MHC-1 and MHC-2, so that they can activate more cytotoxic T cells. Th1 cells also make interferon gamma. Interferon gamma binds to infected cells and blocks virus replication. Th1 cells also signal the infected cells to make more MHC-1, so that they can present more virus peptide to killer cells. All of these functions are inhibited when vIL-10 inactivates Th1 cells.

As vIL-10 blocks cytokine production by Th1 cells, it stimulates Th2 cells to make cytokines that activate B cells. Th2 cytokines further suppress Th1 activity. Activated B cells more easily produce new virus particles. vIL-10 production by infected cells gives EBV a chance to infect more B cells and avoid detection inside its host cells.

PREVENTING CELL DEATH

EBV infection prevents B cells from undergoing apoptosis, programmed cell death, which is normal for all lymphocytes. It does so by inducing the B cell to make a host cell protein called bcl-2. Bcl-2 normally prevents B cells from dying prematurely, but over-production of bcl-2 prevents B cells from dying at the end of their normal life span. Because cytotoxic T cells and NK cells induce apoptosis to kill virus-infected cells, B cells over-producing bcl-2 are also resistant to destruction by NK and cytotoxic T cells. Over-production of bcl-2 maintains infected B cells in the body and increases the chance that reactivation of EBV production will allow virus transfer to a new host.

In addition to bcl-2 production, EBV may inactivate tumor suppressor genes called p53 and Rb. Tumor suppressor

DOES A VIRAL INFECTION CAUSE DIABETES?

There are dozens of autoimmune diseases in which the body's immune system attacks its own tissue. In most cases, it is not known what triggers the start of the disease. In the case of autoimmune or type-1 diabetes, a virus is almost certainly the culprit, although the way in which this occurs is not clear.

Type-1 diabetes, also called juvenile-onset or insulin-dependent diabetes, is usually diagnosed in children and teenagers, but can strike people at any age. Type-1 diabetes is caused by the destruction of beta islet cells in the pancreas that produce insulin. Insulin is a hormone that helps cells take up sugar, which they need for energy. People with type-1 diabetes must inject insulin several times a day. Type-1 diabetes cannot be prevented or cured by eating a sensible diet and remaining slim, as can type-2 diabetes, or adult-onset diabetes.

Common childhood virus infections activate the immune system to make cytotoxic T cells that recognize and kill infected cells. One possible way in which this infection might cause type-1 diabetes is that cytotoxic T cells specific for the virus also recognize uninfected beta islet cells in the pancreas and kill them. Another possibility is that the inflammation caused by virus-specific T cells killing infected cells might induce other T cells to kill uninfected islet cells of the pancreas.

Type-1 diabetes is found more often in people who have an altered form of one of the MHC-2 molecules, DQ-beta 8. Altered DQ-beta 8 molecules do not kill immature T cells, recognizing self-antigens as efficiently as they should. The reason is that immature self-specific T cells must bind self-peptides on MHC to be killed. The altered DQ-beta 8 is unstable, and it cannot bind and present self-peptides to the self-specific T cells. Those T cells mature and, if activated by virus antigen or by an inflammatory response, they can kill beta islet cells.

genes block a cell from dividing uncontrollably. The virus also somehow stabilizes the telomeres (DNA ends), which usually shorten as the cell divides. Shortening of the telomeres may be linked to cell death. Lengthening the lifespan of a cell is called **immortalization**, one of the steps in the process for a cell to become a cancer cell.

7

Diagnosis of Infectious Mononucleosis

The severe sore throat, swollen lymph nodes, and fatigue lasting for 1 to 4 weeks, especially in someone 15 to 24 years old, usually leads the physician to suspect infectious mononucleosis. Two kinds of laboratory tests are generally used to confirm the diagnosis: blood cell counts and tests for antibodies. These tests measure the body's immune response to the virus. Epstein-Barr virus (EBV) can be detected directly and grown in tissue culture, but those tests are too time-consuming and expensive to be used routinely.

BLOOD CELL COUNTS

Blood contains red blood cells (**RBCs**) and white blood cells (leukocytes). The RBCs carry oxygen from the lungs to the tissues and carbon dioxide from the tissues to be exhaled in the lungs. Leukocytes belong to the immune system. They are divided into granulocytes, monocytes, and lymphocytes based on how they appear under the microscope (Figure 7.1).

Granulocytes have a granular appearance and lobed nuclei. They are divided into neutrophils, eosinophils, and basophils based on their colors when stained with the dyes hematoxylin and eosin. Neutrophils (NEWT-row-fills) are the most common cell in the blood. They are phagocytes and are attracted to infection sites by macrophage cytokines. Like macrophages, neutrophils have membrane receptors that allow them to bind common bacterial surface molecules and antibody-coated bacteria and viruses. Once in the tissues, neutrophils rapidly engulf and destroy pathogens. When neutrophils get killed in the line of duty, they form the

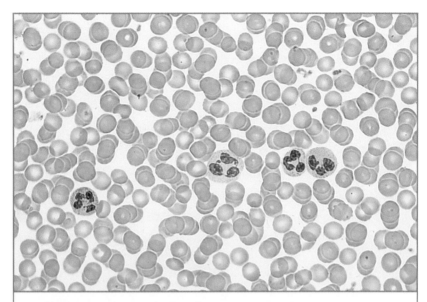

Figure 7.1 Certain white blood cells usually increase in number during an infection. This picture shows four neutrophils with lobed nuclei among the red blood cells. These abnormal neutrophils are common with EBV.

pus that we often see in bacterial infections. Macrophage cytokines signal the bone marrow to make more neutrophils. An elevated white blood cell count usually reflects increased numbers of neutrophils recruited to fight an infection. Eosinophils and basophils are some of the cells that release histamine during an allergic response.

Monocytes are macrophages that travel in the blood. They are rounder than tissue macrophages, and they have round nuclei. Like tissue macrophages, they are phagocytes that can engulf and kill pathogens. They also carry pathogen peptides on their MHC molecules to the lymph nodes, where they activate the T cells. Very low numbers of dendritic cells are also found in blood. They are called veiled cells because their long dendrites resemble gauzy veils.

The lymphocytes are the T and B cells. They are smaller

than the other leukocytes, but bigger than red blood cells. Most lymphocytes in the blood are resting lymphocytes. They have round nuclei and very little cytoplasm. T and B cells look alike under the microscope, but can be identified by tagging them with fluorescent antibodies to their membrane receptors and counting them in a flow cytometer (see box on page 69).

Leukocyte counts in people who are healthy usually range between 4,300 and 10,800 per cubic millimeter of blood (a cube with sides that are a millimeter long). The table shows that more than half of leukocytes are neutrophils and the rest are mostly lymphocytes. There are many more T cells in the blood than B cells. About two-thirds of the T cells are helper (CD4) T cells and the rest are cytotoxic T cells (CD8). CD4 binds MHC-2, and CD8 binds MHC-1.

Normal Human Leukocyte Counts

Granulocytes	Monocytes	Lymphocytes
Neutrophils: 3,000–5,500	165–600	B cells: 300
Eosinophils: 50–250		CD4 T cells: 500–1,600
Basophils: 20		CD8 T cells: 300–900

A typical white blood cell count for someone with infectious mononucleosis would be 12,000 to 18,000 leukocytes in each cubic millimeter of blood. Counts might go as high as 30,000 to 50,000 leukocytes. Although in infections the numbers of neutrophils usually increase, in infectious mononucleosis the neutrophil counts are often somewhat lower than normal. The numbers of lymphocytes are increased to greater than 50% of leukocytes, and many of the lymphocytes look unusual (atypical). Atypical lymphocytes are larger than resting lymphocytes. Many have clear looking bubbles called vacuoles in their cytoplasm. Their edges are curled, and their nuclei are lobed. If they are examined by flow cytometry, most of the atypical lymphocytes are CD8 cytotoxic T cells. Small decreases in

FLOW CYTOMETRY

A simple microscopic blood test does not provide all the information needed to track the course of some diseases like HIV or leukemia, cancer of the white blood cells. For these diseases, it is important to know the numbers of particular kinds of lymphocytes that look identical under the microscope.

Lymphocytes have different membrane receptors depending on their function. B cells have membrane antibody molecules (Ig) that serve as receptors for antigens. B cells also have a membrane complement receptor CR2, the receptor that EBV uses to infect them. T cells have antigen receptors called TCR. Helper T cells have a molecule called CD4; the human immunodeficiency virus (HIV) uses CD4 to infect helper T cells. Cytotoxic T cells have CD8 on their membranes. CD4 and CD8 allow T cells to bind the MHC-peptide complex on the membranes of antigen-presenting cells or infected cells. All of these molecules are called "markers" because they allow scientists to mark or identify different lymphocyte types.

Antibodies can be made that will bind specifically to these markers. Each antibody is chemically tagged with a **fluorochrome**, a molecule that will glow when hit with light from a laser. Antibody to Ig could be tagged with a green fluorochrome, antibody to CD4 with a red fluorochrome, and antibody to CD8 with an orange fluorochrome.

The antibody-coated cells are then passed through a flow cytometer. In this machine, the cells are pulled single file through a narrow tube to a nozzle that vibrates, shaking off droplets, each containing a single cell. As the droplets fall through the machine, they are hit by laser light. Some of the light bounces off the cells at an angle. This scattered light can be interpreted to measure cell size and bumpiness. Other light is collected and analyzed for its color and brightness. Computer programs process the information to show numbers of each cell type (B, helper T, and killer T) as well as how much marker is on each cell and whether the cells are resting (small and smooth) or activated (larger and bumpier).

Antibodies can also be made to tumor antigens (found only on particular cancer cells) to track the success of chemotherapy and to MHC molecules to do tissue typing for transplantation.

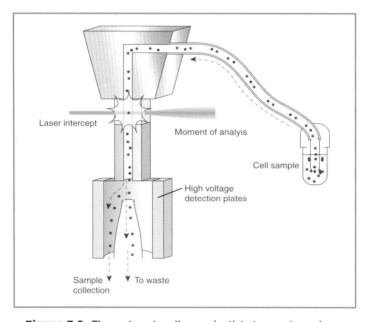

Figure 7.2 Flow cytometry allows scientists to count numbers of cells with certain membrane molecules (markers). Antibodies tagged with fluorochromes bind the cell markers and glow when hit with laser light. Some flow cytometers can also sort cells with different markers into different test tubes. The process of flow cytometry is illustrated here.

platelets, very small cell fragments responsible for clotting, often occur in mononucleosis patients.

Atypical lymphocytes are seen in other diseases: infections with cytomegalovirus (CMV, another herpesvirus), rubella, mumps, and in acute viral hepatitis. They are also seen in certain adverse reactions to drugs.

ANTIBODIES

Two kinds of antibodies are made during an EBV infection. As in all infections, antibodies are made that bind to the infectious agent and help macrophages and neutrophils engulf and kill it. EBV is unusual because it also stimulates B cells to make antibodies that bind to animal red blood cells: heterophile antibodies (literally translated as antibodies that love something else besides the pathogen that induces their production).

Normally, only B cells that bind the pathogen are stimulated to make antibodies. However, because EBV infects B cells and stimulates some of them to divide as they produce more viruses, the infected B cells also make antibodies to whatever antigen they are programmed to recognize. Some of these antibodies will bind sheep, horse, or cow RBCs and cause them to clump together (agglutinate). Between 80 and 85% of people with infectious mononucleosis have these Paul-Bunnell heterophile antibodies, named for their discoverers.

Heterophile antibodies can be detected within the first month of illness. Children are more likely to test negative for heterophile antibodies than are teenagers and adults. There is no correlation between the severity of the mononucleosis and the amount of heterophile antibodies seen, and they gradually disappear from the blood. Heterophile antibodies are also found in CMV infections. CMV infection occurs most often after a blood transfusion, since CMV (like EBV) can remain latent in white blood cells and is not accompanied by a sore throat or swollen lymph nodes.

The Monospot test is used to test for heterophile antibodies. In the Monospot test, horse or cow RBCs are suspended in saline (salt water) on a microscope slide. A few drops of serum from the patient are added to the blood cell suspension. If heterophile antibodies are present, they will bind to the RBCs.

Some antibodies bind adjacent cells with the two arms of the Y, holding the RBCs close together. If enough heterophile antibody is present, the RBCs clump together on the slide: this is a positive heterophile antibody test. False negative tests in a person who has EBV may occur if the levels of heterophile antibodies are so low that no red blood cell clumping occurs.

Antibodies to EBV viral capsid antigen (VCA) are produced in the first few weeks of infection. The stem of the Y-shaped antibody comes in several varieties or classes; different classes have different functions in the body. The IgM class is always made first in an infection. IgM is made of five identical antibody Ys joined at their stems into a starfish shape. It has 10 binding sites with which to grab antigens and is very efficient at agglutinating antigens and at promoting movement of leukocytes to the infection site and phagocytosis of the pathogen. IgM to VCA is seen in the first weeks of infection and disappears after four to six weeks.

As B cells become more activated, they switch to making IgG antibody. IgG is only a single Y, so it can move more easily through the leaky blood vessels into the tissues. IgG antibody to VCA is maximal at four to six weeks of infection. Levels then drop, but IgG to VCA can be detected throughout the lifetime of someone with EBV and is responsible for their being seropositive (having detectable antibodies to EBV). IgG antibody can pass through the placenta and confer passive EBV immunity to the newborn. Other IgG antibody binds to the spike proteins on the EBV envelope and blocks the virus from infecting new cells: this is called **neutralizing antibody**. Weeks after the infection began, antibody to EBNA-1 (Epstein-Barr nuclear antigen) can be detected. Remember that the EBNA-1 molecule prevents EBV DNA from being lost from the nuclei of latently infected B cells.

The most commonly used test for antibody is the **ELISA** (enzyme-linked immunosorbent assay, Figure 7.4). A blood

BLOOD TYPING USING AGGLUTINATION

We all have membrane sugars and proteins on our red blood cells. The sugars are called either Type A or Type B and one of the proteins is called Rh (for the Rhesus monkey in which these molecules were first discovered). Blood with only the A sugar on the RBC is called Type A. Blood with only the B sugar is called

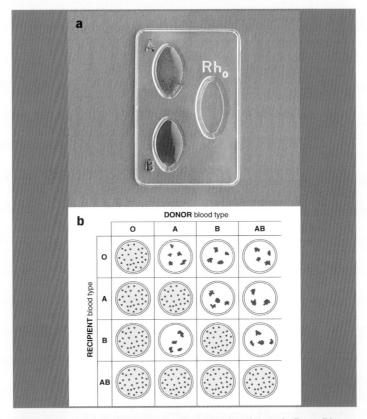

Figure 7.3 Blood cells are mixed with antibodies to A, B, or Rh on a slide and examined for agglutination (top). Notice the agglutination in the well-labeled "a." The lower diagram (b) indicates whether antibodies in the recipient blood can agglutinate the cells in the donor blood. Agglutination is indicated by large clumps of cells, while cells that do not agglutinate are shown evenly distributed in the circle.

Type B. Blood with RBCs bearing both A and B sugars is called Type AB. Blood with RBCs that have neither sugar is called Type O. RBCs with the Rh antigen are called Rh positive (Rh+). RBCs without the Rh antigen are called Rh negative (Rh-).

When someone needs a blood transfusion, his or her blood must be matched with the blood of the donor. The reason for matching is that the blood also contains antibodies. The intestines have live bacteria called **normal flora**. The bacteria do not harm, but occasionally a few may enter the lymphoid tissues of the intestines. Antibodies are made to the sugars on their surfaces that are identical to the A and B sugars on the RBC. Because B cells that make antibodies to "self" antigens are killed before they mature, someone with type A RBCs will have only antibody to type B sugar. Someone with type B RBCs has antibody to type A sugar. Someone with type AB blood has no antibodies. Someone with type O blood (no A or B sugars) has antibodies to both A and B.

Blood Type	Sugars on RBC	Antibodies in Serum
A	A	Anti-B
B	B	Anti-A
AB	A and B	None
O	Neither A nor B	Anti-A and Anti-B

If someone with type A blood were to get Type B blood, their anti-B antibodies would agglutinate the Type B RBCs. Agglutinated RBCs would block the capillaries, and no blood could get to their tissues. Blood type must also be matched in organ donation because many cells in the body have the same A and B antigens as the RBCs.

Blood typing or cross matching is generally done by slide agglutination tests similar to the Monospot test (Figure 7.3a). Antibodies to A, B, and Rh are mixed with the blood on separate slides. If the blood agglutinates with anti-A, it is Type B blood. If it agglutinates with B, it is Type A, and so forth. If it agglutinates with anti-Rh, it is Rh positive. If it does not agglutinate, it is Rh negative. Because there are many other blood typing antigens, the safety of a blood transfusion can be checked by directly mixing blood from both donor and recipient on the same slide. If no agglutination occurs, the transfusion can take place (Figure 7.3b).

sample from the patient is allowed to clot, and the straw-colored fluid around the clot is the **serum**. EBV grown in the laboratory and a sample of patient serum are combined in a special dish. If EBV-specific antibodies are present in the patient serum, they will stick to the virus on the surface of the dish, while other serum proteins, heterophile antibodies, and antibodies made in other infections will be washed away. Antibodies that are specific for (bind to) the patient antibodies are then added. These **secondary antibodies** are chemically linked to enzymes. Finally, colorless substrate molecules are added and are changed into colored products by the enzymes. The presence of color shows that the patient has antibody to EBV. Instead of whole virus, certain virus proteins can be used to identify antibodies to VCA, early antigen, or EBNA.

Because the IgG antibody to EBV can be found in everyone who has ever been infected, it is not proof by itself that a disease the patient has now is caused by EBV. Chapter 10 discusses chronic fatigue syndrome, which was once thought to be caused by EBV.

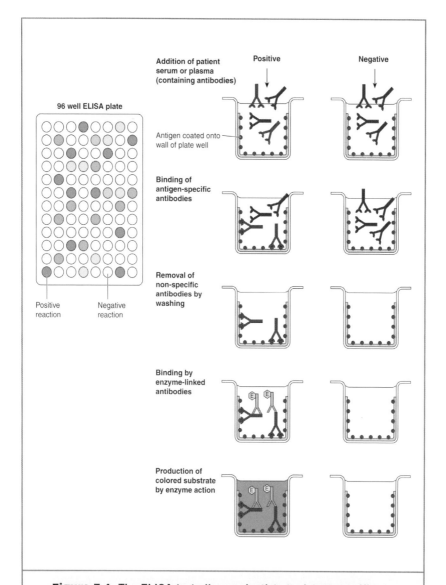

Figure 7.4 The ELISA test allows scientists to detect specific antibodies that bind EBV antigens. Pure EBV is coated onto plastic wells and patient serum is added. If the patient has antibodies to EBV, enzyme-linked secondary antibodies bind and the enzyme converts colorless molecules into colored molecules. The diagram above shows both positive and negative results.

VIRUS CULTURE

EBV can be recovered from the throat of someone who is infected by having him or her gargle with salt water and collecting the fluid. A small piece of infected lymph node that is ground up in fluid will also release viruses. The fluid containing the viruses is passed through a filter with pores 0.45 micrometers in diameter to remove any bacteria and cell pieces that are present. The fluid is then added to tissue culture with cells that can serve as hosts for EBV: epithelial cells or B cells. The virus will replicate in the tissue culture cells and can be identified under the electron microscope. This test takes days to weeks to perform and is expensive, so it is not routinely done for EBV diagnosis.

PCR

Polymerase chain reaction (**PCR**) is a more sensitive technique than culture for detecting and identifying EBV. The process involves using small pieces of EBV DNA, called **primers**. The primers are added to blood or lymph node cells that might contain EBV DNA. Cycles of heating and cooling the DNA allow the primers to hybridize (match up) with identical pathogen DNA so that enzymes called **DNA polymerases** can make copies. DNA that does not match the primers will not be copied, so only EBV DNA will be made. Once enough copying cycles have occurred, the DNA can be detected by hybridizing it with radioactive EBV DNA. Although PCR is faster than tissue culture, it is expensive and is not performed routinely to diagnose EBV infection.

8

Treatments for Infectious Mononucleosis

TREATING THE SYMPTOMS

Almost all people with healthy immune systems recover from infectious mononucleosis without any treatment. Gargling with salt water eases throat pain. Anti-inflammatory medications, such as acetaminophen or ibuprofen, can be taken to reduce fever and sore throat pain. Aspirin should not be taken by anyone under 16 years of age, because it can cause a rare, but serious nervous system complication called Reye's (rye) syndrome. The usual prescribed treatment for mononucleosis involves bed rest during the first week or two when symptoms are most severe and avoiding blows to the abdomen for several weeks. Isolation from other people is usually not necessary, but avoiding kissing or sharing eating utensils is a sensible precaution against spreading the disease.

For someone with tonsils so enlarged that they block the airways, or for a severe decline in RBCs or platelet numbers, corticosteroids may be given. Corticosteroids, such as prednisone, reduce the activity of the immune system. Because tonsil inflammation resulting from the death of EBV-infected B cells and production of heterophile antibodies that destroy blood cells are immune system functions, inhibiting the immune system relieves the complications. Medication levels must be high enough to reduce symptoms but low enough so that the immune response can still eliminate EBV. Corticosteroids have serious side effects, especially when taken for long periods of time, so they are not used routinely.

Antibiotics are chemicals made by microorganisms (naturally occurring) that kill or block the growth of other microorganisms. Microbes use antibiotics to compete for space and food. Penicillin is an antibiotic produced by a mold, *Penicillium notatum,* a common blue-green mold that can be seen growing on bread (Figure 8.1). The British **microbiologist** Sir Alexander Fleming (Figure 8.2) discovered penicillin in 1929 when he noticed that a colony of mold growing on one of his bacterial cultures had a ring around it in which none of his bacteria could grow. Howard Florey and Ernst Chain at Oxford University later purified penicillin, for which they received the Nobel Prize in Physiology or Medicine with Fleming in 1945.

REYE'S SYNDROME

Reye's (pronounced "rye") syndrome is a reaction in children younger than 16 years to aspirin during and after a viral infection. Taking aspirin or other medications containing salicylate (an ingredient of aspirin) soon after chicken pox or flu-like infections causes abnormal accumulation of fat in the liver and brain swelling.

Reye's syndrome affects only one in a million children. It occurs most frequently in winter during the flu season. Since warning labels were placed on salicylate-containing medications in 1988, the number of cases has dropped. Reye's syndrome has been reported to occur after infection with influenza, chicken pox, mumps, rubella, measles, polio, EBV, herpes simplex, cytomegalovirus (CMV), coxsackie A and B, and adenovirus 2 and 3.

Reye's syndrome begins with vomiting, fatigue, moodiness, nausea, and loss of energy. It progresses to personality changes, confusion, and restlessness, and possibly coma and convulsions. Early diagnosis and treatment leads to a 90% chance of recovery. Without early treatment, half of all sufferers die.

Figure 8.1 The antibiotic penicillin is produced from a blue-green mold called *Penicillium notatum*. This mold generally grows on bread. A close-up of *Penicillium notatum* is shown here.

Penicillin was first commercially produced in the United States during World War II and saved many military troops from dying of infection.

Most of the antibiotics currently used come from the mold family *Streptomyces*. They produce the antibiotics streptomycin, erythromycin, neomycin, tetracycline, and gentamycin. The molds *Penicillium notatum* and *Cephalosporium* produce the antibiotics penicillin, griseofulvin, and cephalothin, and two species of *Bacillus* produce bacitracin and polymixin.

Figure 8.2 Sir Alexander Fleming, shown here in his laboratory, discovered penicillin in 1929. Fleming was culturing bacteria when he noticed that a mold had infected his culture plates. Bacteria did not grow around the area where the mold was present.

Antimicrobials are chemicals synthesized in the laboratory (artificial) to kill or block the growth of **microbes**. Many are adaptations of naturally occurring antibiotics, but others are completely new drugs.

Bacteria are microscopic organisms about one-tenth the size of human cells. They are surrounded by a cell membrane and by a rigid cell wall that gives them a characteristic shape. They do not have organelles, such as mitochondria and Golgi, in their cytoplasm, but they have their own enzymes that perform all the chemical reactions they need to live. Often some of these enzymes differ enough from those of humans that they can be used as the target of antibiotics.

Antibiotics and antimicrobials act on bacteria in several ways. Some block cell wall synthesis. Because this process occurs in bacteria, but not in humans or animals, these antibiotics usually have few side effects. Some antibiotics block the production of other nutrients essential to bacteria, but not to mammals. Other antibiotics block protein synthesis. Because the cell machinery for making proteins is different in bacteria and in mammals, these antibiotics also have few side effects. Antibiotics that interfere with the structure of the cell membrane have been effective against molds, whose cell membranes have different lipids than mammalian membranes. Antibiotics that block DNA synthesis often interfere with mammalian cell enzymes and have the highest incidence of side effects.

Because viruses use host cell enzymes to produce new viruses, only antimicrobials that interfere with host cell enzyme functions are effective against virus infections, and these antimicrobials have serious side effects. Antibiotics such as penicillin that are designed to interfere with bacterial enzymes are useless against virus infections. In fact, most people with mononucleosis who are given the antibiotic ampicillin develop a nonallergic skin rash. In most cases of virus infection, the body must depend on the immune system to kill the viruses.

ANTIVIRAL DRUGS

Medications used to treat viral infections are designed to block enzymes that are required to produce viruses, but not human proteins. Many antiviral drugs target viruses that have RNA for their genetic information, such as influenza virus or HIV. RNA viruses must have enzymes that can copy RNA to make more **genomes** for the new viruses. HIV has an enzyme, reverse transcriptase, which copies RNA into DNA. HIV then integrates the DNA into the host cell DNA. The presence of reverse transcriptase gave rise to the name retroviruses (reverse viruses) for the group of viruses that includes HIV. Because human cells do not have RNA copying enzymes, drugs that interfere with their activity can be effective against these viruses.

EBV is a DNA virus, and it uses host cell enzymes to copy its DNA into new virus DNA and transcribe it into messenger RNA. For this reason, medications that block EBV replication would also block host cell production of messenger RNA and new DNA. These drugs would act like anticancer drugs and cause the same serious side effects: reduced immune system function, decreased production of both red blood cells and leukocytes, loss of hair, and nausea from damage to the intestinal lining. In uncomplicated mononucleosis, antiviral drugs do not shorten the course of the disease.

White blood cells and infected cells make interferons during a virus infection. Interferon alpha blocks the production of the virus, while interferon gamma activates antigen-presenting cells and cytotoxic T cells (Figure 8.3). These drugs have been produced in the laboratory and can be given to patients whose immune systems are weakened. They cause side effects when given in high doses and are expensive, so interferons are not used in typical cases of mononucleosis.

Giving antibodies isolated from the blood of healthy people (called **intravenous** Ig or **IVIG**) inhibits antibody production by the EBV-infected person's B cells. IVIG is given when heterophile antibodies cause severe depletion of platelets. Because IVIG also blocks production of antibodies to EBV that neutralize the virus and promote its phagocytosis, IVIG is not routinely given.

PREVENTION

Because acquiring EBV infection early in life usually results in fewer symptoms than when it is acquired later, and because infection is so common, preventing EBV infection or reinfection

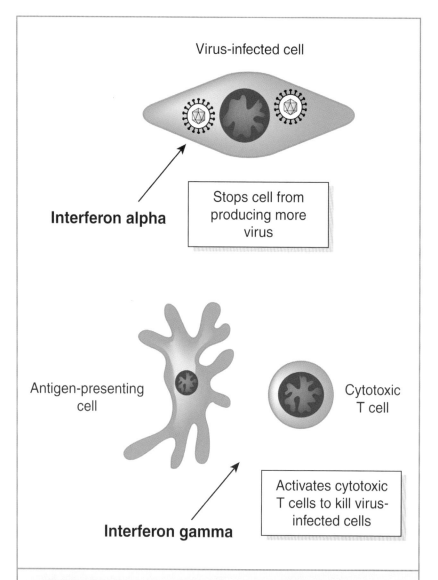

Figure 8.3 The immune system has many methods to prevent reinfection by a virus. One of those methods is illustrated here. Interferon alpha is made by infected cells and blocks virus production in nearby cells. Interferon gamma is produced by helper T cells and stimulates cytotoxic T cells to kill infected cells.

is important only in people whose immune systems are weakened. Someone with symptomatic infectious mononucleosis should not donate blood because the virus will be present in the blood and can infect or reinfect the recipients of the blood.

Vaccines have not been developed for EBV or other herpesviruses. People who have a weakened immune system and are at risk for serious disease if infected by EBV would be endangered by being vaccinated with a live but weakened (**attenuated**) virus. The link between EBV and cancer also causes concern about vaccinating with live virus. Even a weakened virus might be able to become latent in B cells and eventually transform them into tumor cells. Vaccinating with killed virus or with purified virus proteins does not induce the strong cytotoxic T cell memory that is necessary to prevent mononucleosis symptoms.

New vaccines are being studied that involve the injection of virus DNA into muscle cells. The muscle cells respond by producing pathogen proteins that stimulate the immune system. DNA vaccines in animals induce both antibody and cytotoxic T cell production with no harm to the vaccinated animal. The genes in EBV DNA that allow the virus to become latent or to transform cells could be removed, leaving only the genes for VCA (**virus capsid antigen**) and spike protein that would induce protective immunity.

9

Epstein-Barr Virus and Cancer

WHAT IS CANCER?

Cancer (Figure 9.1) is uncontrolled cell proliferation. Cells in the body normally divide only when they receive specific signals from growth factors or cytokines. When the signals disappear, the cells stop proliferating. If cells continue to divide even in the absence of specific signals, they form a collection of cancer cells called a **tumor**. A slow-growing tumor that stays in its original location is **benign** (be-NINE) (harmless) unless it becomes so large that it presses on nearby tissues. Even benign tumors in the brain are dangerous because there is no room for the tumor to grow. **Malignant** tumors have cancer cells that travel to distant sites in the blood. The skin tumor melanoma becomes deadly when it spreads to the lungs and brain. Spread of cancer cells to distant sites is called **metastasis**.

The conversion of a normal cell into a cancer cell requires several steps. We know this from watching cells in the colon become colon cancer cells. For example, cells in the colon that become colon cancer cells will first begin to divide, forming growths called polyps (poll-ips) in the lining of the large intestine. If the polyps are removed, cancer is prevented. If the polyps are allowed to grow, some of the cells become metastatic and travel to other organs. Metastatic cancer cannot be cured by surgery because collections of tumor cells too small to see are spread throughout the body. At this point, chemotherapy and radiation must be used to kill the tumor cells.

Cancer is caused by exposure to chemicals, radiation, and viruses,

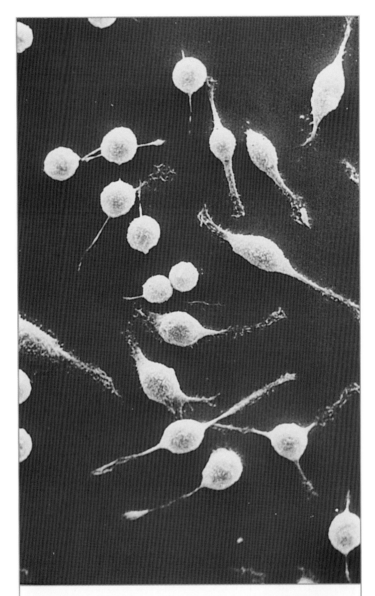

Figure 9.1 Cancer is a disease that causes cells to grow unhindered. When a large number of these cells collect in one area, they form a tumor. This electron micrograph shows cancer cells in a human culture, stained yellow for better visibility.

which are called **carcinogens**, or cancer-causing agents. All of these agents damage the DNA so that normal cells become **transformed** into cancer cells. The longer a person lives, the more likely the person is to suffer damage to his or her DNA that could result in cancer. Fortunately, some cancer cells have abnormal peptides on their MHC-1 and can be recognized and killed by NK cells and cytotoxic T cells.

CANCER-CAUSING VIRUSES

Peyton Rous (Figure 9.2) discovered a chicken cancer caused by a virus in 1911. Remember that in 1911, the electron microscope had not yet been invented, and people knew little about viruses except that they were small enough to pass through Chamberland filters. They did know that tumors were caused by rapidly proliferating cells and that they appeared spontaneously (without apparent cause).

Rous was a pathologist at the Rockefeller Institute in New York. The cancer he was studying was a sarcoma, cancer of the muscle. Rous decided to see if he could transfer the tumor from one chicken to another. He ground up some of the tumor cells and passed them through a filter. Then, he injected the clear fluid into other chickens. Some of those chickens also got sarcomas (tumors). Rous could grind up the new tumors and cause sarcoma in still more chickens. Sarcoma behaved like an infectious disease. Because only about half of the injected chickens got sarcomas, Rous's work was ignored. However, when the virus causing the tumors was eventually identified, it was named Rous sarcoma virus (RSV) after him.

It was not until 1958 that Howard Temin grew RSV in chick embryos and demonstrated that the virus transformed normal cells into cancer cells. Howard Temin and David Baltimore independently isolated reverse transcriptase, the enzyme that copies RNA into DNA, from RSV in 1970. They shared the Nobel Prize in Physiology or Medicine for their

Figure 9.2 Dr. Peyton Rous, shown here, discovered a virus that causes cancer in chickens in 1911. He found that by transferring some tumor cells from one chicken to another, he could induce cancer in some of the chickens that received the cells.

work. The discovery of reverse transcriptase made gene cloning and genetic engineering possible. RSV is a retrovirus, just like HIV. By integrating its DNA into muscle cells, it transforms them into tumor cells.

In humans, viruses cause several tumors. Papillomavirus is a DNA virus that causes genital warts. Certain papillomaviruses have been linked to cervical cancer. Recently, a vaccine for papillomavirus was shown to be very effective at preventing genital warts and cancer. Hepatitis B and C viruses (HBV and HCV) can cause liver cancer. HTLV-1 (human T cell leukemia virus), a relative of HIV, causes T cell tumors. Human herpesvirus-8 causes Kaposi's sarcoma, a disease of pigmented epithelial cells that is more common in people infected with HIV.

Viruses cause cancers in several ways. They may induce the production of virus proteins that cause the host cell to begin proliferating or prevent it from dying. They may insert their DNA into the host cell DNA at a location that causes the overproduction of host cell proteins associated with cell division. Viruses may also carry viral **oncogenes**: cancer-causing genes that mimic growth factors by stimulating cell division. Viral oncogenes are usually genes taken from host cells by viruses and introduced into new cells. If they are inserted into the host cell DNA in a new location, they may become cancer-causing by stimulating host cell proliferation.

HOW EBV CAUSES CANCER

Although it is not exactly known how EBV causes cancer, EBV DNA can be found in cells from several kinds of cancer: Burkitt's lymphoma, nasopharyngeal carcinoma, and some Hodgkin's lymphomas. A **lymphoma** is a solid tumor of leukocytes, while a **leukemia** is a "liquid" tumor in which the cancerous leukocytes circulate in the blood. Burkitt's lymphoma and EBV-containing Hodgkin's lymphomas are B cell cancers. Nasopharyngeal carcinoma is a cancer of the epithelial cells behind the throat and above the roof of the mouth.

In all cancers caused by EBV, virus DNA is present in the tumor cells. In 90% of cases, tumor cells also have a **chromosomal translocation**: the end of chromosome 8 has been exchanged with the end of chromosome 14. This

VACCINATING AGAINST CANCER

There are few cancers for which a vaccine has been made, although all anticancer vaccines are still experimental and not used routinely on humans. One of the most promising of these is the vaccine against human papillomavirus (HPV).

HPV is a DNA virus that causes genital warts. HPV remains in the wart cells and sometimes the warts develop into cervical cancer. Papillomaviruses infect 5.5 million Americans annually, compared to one million people who become infected with genital herpes each year. More than 75% of adults in developed countries are infected with HPV. There are more than 100 types of HPV, but only a few cause genital warts (HPV-6 and HPV-11) and cancer (HPV-16 and HPV-18).

In October 2002, the pharmaceutical company Merck and Company announced results from clinical trials of an HPV vaccine. Of more than 750 women who received the HPV-16 vaccine, none became infected with HPV-16. In the same-sized control group of women who received no vaccine, 41 women were infected with HPV-16.

Additional trials by Merck and other companies are in progress to test a vaccine against all four HPV types that cause genital warts or cancer. It is too early to tell if any of the vaccines will prevent cervical cancer, but the day may come when routine Pap smears, the test used to detect precancerous or cancer cells on the cervix, can be replaced by a series of vaccinations.

translocation brings the gene *c-myc* on chromosome 8 close to the genes for antibody on chromosome 22.

The gene *c-myc* is a gene for a protein required for cell division. It is a proto-oncogene, a gene that causes cancer when it is activated. The antibody gene region is "turned on" in B cells, which means antibody messenger RNA is actively produced. When *c-myc* is translocated into the antibody gene region, the *c-myc* protein is also actively produced. The cell divides uncontrollably, becoming a cancer cell. The bcl-2 protein that blocks apoptosis (programmed cell death) is also overproduced when its gene is translocated into the antibody gene region of B cells (Figure 9.3).

Burkitt's lymphoma is a very rapidly growing cancer that can be successfully treated with chemotherapy. The chemotherapy drugs interfere with DNA synthesis in the rapidly dividing cancer cells. Common side effects of hair loss, nausea, and increased susceptibility to infection are caused by the drugs' effects on the rapidly dividing cells of the hair follicles, intestinal lining, and immune system.

COCARCINOGENS

The geographical data collected by Denis Burkitt (Chapter 2) showed that Burkitt's lymphoma occurs in a particular insect habitat. The insect is the mosquito, which transmits malaria and many other diseases.

Malaria is caused by a single-celled parasite called *Plasmodium falciparum* and its close relatives. *Plasmodium* sporozoites enter the bloodstream through a mosquito bite and infect liver cells. In the liver, *Plasmodium* sporozoites become merozoites that infect red blood cells. Periodically the infected RBCs rupture, releasing more merozoites and toxins that cause fever and chills (Figure 9.4). Because RBCs have no MHC-1, NK and cytotoxic T cells cannot kill them. Infected RBCs stick to capillary walls before they reach the spleen, where Kupffer cells could remove them. Loss of RBCs results in fatigue and

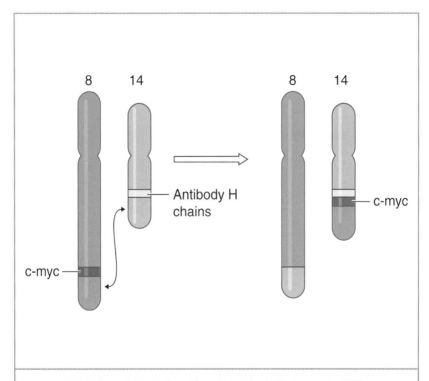

8   14   8   14

c-myc

Antibody H
chains

c-myc

c-myc

Figure 9.3 Occasionally, although rarely, infection with EBV causes part of chromosome 8 to move to chromosome 14. This process is illustrated here. When this occurs, proteins are over-produced that cause the cell to become a cancer cell.

shortness of breath. Small children are at highest risk of death from malaria because of severe anemia.

Plasmodium falciparum suppresses the ability of dendritic cells to present antigens to T cells and initiate an immune response. Suppression of immune responses in children with malaria is thought to allow EBV to infect more B cells without being killed. The higher EBV antibody levels in children with Burkitt's lymphoma is probably caused by the inability of their T cells to kill EBV-infected B cells. Because malaria greatly increases a child's chances of getting Burkitt's lymphoma, malaria is called a cocarcinogen, a cancer-causing agent.

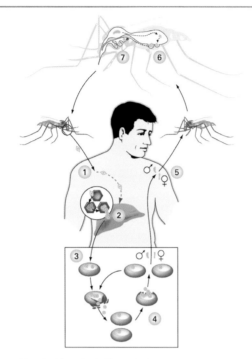

1. Mosquito infected with *Plasmodium* bites human.
   Plasmodium from mosquito salivary glands enters bloodstream.

2. *Plasmodium* invades hepatocytes in the liver and starts to reproduce.

3. *Plasmodium* enters red blood cells.

4. Further reproduction of the parasite causes red blood cells to burst.
   Other red blood cells become infected.
   Cycles of red blood cell infection and destruction coincide with fever
   and chills.

5. Mosquito bites human and picks up *Plasmodium* reproductive cells.

6. *Plasmodium* reproduces.

7. *Plasmodium* migrates to mosquito salivary glands.

Figure 9.4 *Plasmodium falciparum*, the organism that causes malaria, has a complex life cycle, as can be seen in this diagram. First, the *Plasmodium* enters the human bloodstream while a mosquito is feeding on the blood, travels to the liver, and reproduces. Then it leaves the liver and continues to replicate in red blood cells, causing them to burst, thus releasing the parasite into the bloodstream where it can be picked up by another mosquito feeding on the blood of the infected person.

The cocarcinogen for nasopharyngeal carcinoma is unknown. It might be a chemical from the salted fish that is common in the diet in the geographical regions where the carcinoma occurs. Another possibility is that people in those regions have MHC-1 types that make it difficult for their cytotoxic T cells to recognize EBV peptides.

10

Epstein-Barr Virus and Other Diseases

CHRONIC FATIGUE SYNDROME

A few days after she had a wisdom tooth extracted, Karen thought she might still be feeling the effects of the anesthesia. She did not feel ill, just exhausted and depressed. The fatigue dragged on for weeks. Occasionally, her throat would hurt or her muscles would ache.[2]

When Karen finally went to her physician, the physician could find nothing wrong with her. The physician suggested Karen might have the flu and could not explain why she had felt tired for several months.

Karen began to read of other cases like hers in newspapers and magazines. The disease received a tentative diagnosis—chronic EBV infection. The newspapers called it "yuppie flu" or "affluenza" because most of the sufferers were professionals between 20 and 40 years old. Some suggested that the people who complained of the illness were overachievers who were unconsciously looking for a way off the fast track.

An outbreak of chronic fatigue in Lake Tahoe, on the California-Nevada border, in 1985 became the subject of an episode of the ABC television show *20/20*. The Centers for Disease Control and Prevention, the public health agency of the federal government that tracks disease outbreaks, sent two investigators to interview patients and take blood samples. Of 134 patients interviewed, 15 were identified as most likely to have chronic EBV infection. The patients had persistent or recurring unexplained fatigue that lasted for at least two months and kept them from daily activities for at least two weeks. Other symptoms in some patients were recurring low-grade fever, sore throat, muscle aches, and headaches.

An enlarged spleen was found in 13 of the patients. Thirteen of the 15 patients were female; their ages ranged from 13 to 52.

Results of serological tests were published in the *Morbidity and Mortality Weekly Report*, the weekly publication of the Centers for Disease Control and Prevention. Available at www.cdc.gov, this publication tracks notifiable diseases in all 50 states. The 15 patients were compared with 118 other patients who had been tested for EBV antibodies. The case patients were more likely to have higher antibody **titers** (amounts) to EBV early antigen and capsid antigen (VCA). They also had higher antibody titers to CMV and herpes simplex virus-1. However, there was considerable overlap in the antibody titers between the patients and the general population, so many people without symptoms had antibody titers as high as those in the patients. Because of variability in antibody measurements between laboratories and the nonspecific symptoms, EBV was not proved to be the cause of the disease.

Nearly 20 years later, the cause of chronic fatigue syndrome (CFS) has not been discovered. The disease begins with a low-grade fever, sore throat, muscle aches, and overwhelming fatigue, just like the start of many virus infections. In the second stage, patients have memory problems, trouble concentrating, loss of balance, and bouts of fatigue. No single infectious agent has been found in people with CFS. The National Institutes of Health is currently recruiting patients for a research study on chronic fatigue syndrome. Visit its web site at http://clinicaltrials.gov to see how patients are recruited for clinical trials.

BONE MARROW TRANSPLANTATION AND EBV

Bone marrow transplantation (Figure 10.1) replaces the entire blood-forming system in the body. Cells called **stem cells** in the bone marrow respond to growth and differentiation signals by proliferating and differentiating into red blood cells and

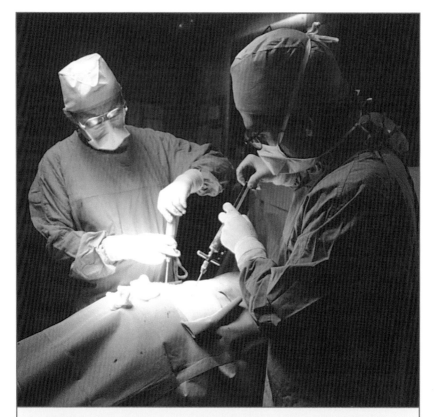

Figure 10.1 Bone marrow transplantation replaces all blood-forming cells. Marrow is removed from the hip bones of the donor using large syringes (shown here) and given like a blood transfusion to the recipient.

all of the leukocyte types. Billions of new cells are made daily as billions of old cells die by apoptosis or are removed by the Kupffer cells.

Bone marrow transplantation is usually performed for two reasons: to replace defective stem cells with healthy ones and to eliminate leukemia, cancer of the leukocytes. In someone whose stem cells were defective at birth or stopped working later in life, anemia is the problem. Anemia is low levels of one or several types of blood cells. If RBC levels are low, too little oxygen is carried to the tissues. If leukocytes cannot be made, infections occur. If a leukocyte has become a cancer cell, the high numbers of cancer cells in the blood prevent the marrow from making normal cells to fight infection. Leukemias can occur in granulocytes, monocytes, and lymphocytes.

To prevent rejection during a transplant, donor bone marrow must be found that has the same MHC proteins as in the patient. Once a matching marrow has been found, the patient is treated with drugs and medication to kill all stem cells (and leukemia cells). This process makes room in the marrow for the new cells to adhere and begin producing healthy blood cells. It usually takes several weeks before blood cell counts are high enough to protect the patient from infection; during that time she or he is hospitalized in isolation from people who might bring in disease organisms. Antirejection drugs must be taken for the rest of the patient's life unless the marrow comes from an identical twin because there are so many MHC proteins that it is impossible to find a perfect match. Transplantation may fail because the new stem cells do not settle in the marrow and produce blood cells or because of rejection. Because the patient has no immune system, it is the marrow that rejects the patient as "nonself." This is called graft-versus-host disease.

While the new blood cells are being made, there are no memory cytotoxic T cells or NK cells to recognize and control virus infections. Because most people have been infected with EBV, chances are high that the donated marrow contains a few B cells latently infected with EBV. Should EBV be reactivated in these cells and stimulate them to become lymphoma cells, the patient will develop a B cell lymphoma. The link between EBV and post-transplant lymphoma was discovered in the case of a Texas boy who died of the disease after living his whole life in a plastic bubble because he was born without the ability to make T and B cells (see box on page 100).

THE BUBBLE BOY

In 1972, David Vetter was born in Texas. He appeared healthy at birth, but soon developed infection after infection. Blood tests showed that David had **SCID**: severe combined immune deficiency. He had been born without an immune system; there were no T cells or B cells in his blood, and his lymph nodes and spleen were very small. An enzyme that is required for the DNA rearrangements that allow lymphocytes to make specific antigen receptors had malfunctioned, and without it his body was defenseless against infectious diseases.

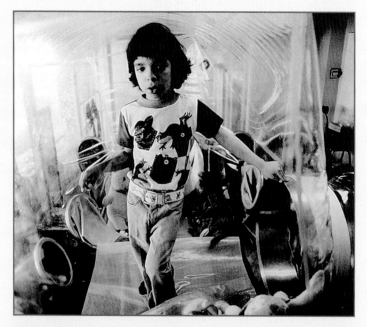

Figure 10.2 David Vetter was known as the "Bubble Boy" because he had to live his life in a sterile bubble. David was born with SCID, or severe combined immune deficiency. His immune system did not function, and because there was no treatment, he had to live in a completely sterile environment because his body would not be able to fend off any invading organisms. David was about four years old in this picture and is surrounded by his bubble.

In 1972, there was no treatment for SCID. David's parents made the choice to raise him in a sterile plastic bubble (Figure 10.2). When he was small, the bubble surrounded his bassinet. Gloves attached to the sides allowed his parents to hold him and care for him. As David grew, the bubble was enlarged so he could walk and play. All food and toys were sterilized before they were put into the bubble, so no stray bacterium or virus would enter.

David lived in the bubble until he was almost 12 years old. NASA donated a suit with its own filtered air supply, so he could occasionally leave the bubble on field trips, but it was too difficult to do often. David grew weary of watching the world through plastic; he wanted a normal life. The doctors suggested a bone marrow transplant. In 1984, bone marrow transplants were not routine, but giving David new blood-forming cells with a healthy enzyme for lymphocyte formation was his one chance of having a normal life.

David received bone marrow from his sister, and everyone watched anxiously. For the first two months, David's blood cell counts did not change. Then, he developed a fever. Within a few days he had diarrhea and was vomiting; his fever went as high as 105°F. He was removed from the bubble, able for the first time to feel the touch of his family. All treatments failed, and 124 days after the transplant David died.

An autopsy showed that he had a B cell cancer, similar to Burkitt's lymphoma. All of the B cells contained EBV. Doctors concluded that the bone marrow cells from David's sister contained a few latently infected B cells. She had contracted EBV early in life and had not become ill. Her healthy immune system controlled the infection. Anytime virus replication was reactivated in her body, her immune system would kill all the virus-producing cells. Even her healthy immune system, however, could not eliminate the few remaining B cells with latent virus that were invisible to her cytotoxic T cells. When those latently infected B cells were put into David's body, he had no cytotoxic T cells with which to control them. One of the cells began to divide and was transformed into a cancer cell, and again David had no T cells with which to kill the cancer. It was the final link between EBV and cancer, and remains a concern today for transplant patients.

Post-transplant lymphoproliferative disease (PTLD) or proliferation of lymphocytes after transplantation can also occur after transplantation of other organs because antirejection drugs suppress T cell activity. For PTLD after bone marrow transplantation, there has been some success after transfusion of mature T cells from the blood of a healthy person. These T cells can control the EBV until the transplant patient makes enough healthy T cells to fight the virus.

AIDS AND EBV

AIDS, acquired immune deficiency syndrome, is caused by the human immunodeficiency virus (HIV). HIV uses CD4 to infect helper T cells. As the CD4 T cells produce HIV, they are unable to participate in immune responses. People infected with HIV usually die of **opportunistic infections**, infections with bacteria or viruses that rarely cause death in people with healthy immune systems.

People infected with HIV also have higher rates of cancer than people with healthy immune systems. EBV is found in one-third of lymphomas occurring in AIDS patients. An early sign of HIV infection in adults is oral hairy leukoplakia. Patients with oral hairy leukoplakia have raised white corrugated areas on the tongue. EBV DNA is present in the cells of those areas. In children with HIV, EBV DNA is sometimes found in the lungs of those suffering from pneumonia when lymphocytes invade the lung tissue. The high incidence of EBV-associated tumors in AIDS patients is undoubtedly due to their suppressed immune systems.

Glossary

Anemia—The reduced ability of blood to carry oxygen that is caused by low levels of red blood cells or hemoglobin.

Antibiotic—A molecule made by one microbe that kills or inhibits the growth of another microbe.

Antibody (pl. **antibodies**)—A protein made by B cells in response to antigen. An antibody specifically binds only the antigen to which it was made.

Antigen—A molecule on a pathogen that the immune system recognizes as foreign.

Antimicrobial (drug)—A laboratory-made drug that kills or blocks the growth of microbes. Often called an antibiotic, although technically antibiotics are made by microbes and antimicrobials are synthesized in the lab.

Apoptosis—Programmed cell death.

ATP—Adenosine triphosphate, the molecule that stores chemical energy from food.

Attenuate—Weaken. An attenuated microbe cannot cause disease.

Autoimmune Disease—A type of disease in which the body's immune system attacks its own tissue. Examples include type-1 diabetes, multiple sclerosis, and rheumatoid arthritis.

B Cell—A type of immune system cell (lymphocyte) that makes an antibody in response to a microbe antigen.

Bacteriophage—A virus that infects bacteria; also called a phage (fage).

Benign (be-NINE) **Tumor**—A tumor that does not spread from its original location and is easily removed.

Budding—The process by which enveloped viruses leave the host cell.

Burkitt's Lymphoma—A tumor in the jaw in which white blood cells are infected with Epstein-Barr virus.

Capsid—A protein coat that surrounds the genetic material of a virus.

Carcinogen—A cancer-causing agent, usually a chemical, radiation, or a virus.

Chromosomal Translocation—The exchange of pieces of two different chromosomes. Chromosomal translocation is associated with Burkitt's lymphoma.

CMV—Cytomegalovirus, a type of herpesvirus that causes a form of mononucleosis.

Contagious—Easy to transmit from one person to another.

Cytokine—(SITE-oh-kine) A chemical signal made by white blood cells.

Cytoplasm—(SITE-oh-plasm) The gel-like material inside cells, surrounded by a membrane.

Cytotoxic T Cell (CTL)—A type of T cell (immune system cell) that recognizes virus-infected host cells and kills them; also called a killer T cell.

Differentiation—Change in cell function. For example, in response to an antigen, resting T and B cells become killer T cells and antibody-producing B cells.

Disease Sign—A change in the body that the physician can see and measure.

Disease Symptom—A change in the body reported by the patient.

DNA—Deoxyribonucleic acid, the chemical that contains all the genetic information of the cell.

DNA Polymerase—An enzyme that copies DNA.

EBV—Epstein-Barr virus, the cause of infectious mononucleosis.

ELISA—A test for antibodies.

Endemic—A disease that is always present in a few people.

Envelope—A phospholipid membrane surrounding the capsid of some viruses; originally part of the host cell plasma membrane.

Enzyme—A protein that catalyzes a chemical reaction inside cells.

Epidemic—A disease outbreak in many people at the same time.

Episome—A circular piece of virus DNA present in the nucleus but separate from the host cell chromosomes.

Erythrocyte—Red blood cells.

Glossary

Fever—A controlled increase in body temperature that helps fight disease.

Fluorochrome—A molecule that will glow when hit with light from a laser.

Genome—The genetic information of a cell or virus. For human cells, the genome is DNA; for viruses it may be DNA or RNA.

Golgi Complex—An organelle, a membrane system inside cells that transports molecules from one location to another.

Granulocyte—A type of leukocyte that has a granular appearance and a lobed nucleus.

Helper T Cell—A type of T cell (immune system cell) that makes cytokines to enable B cells to make antibodies.

Heterophile Antibody—An antibody that is made in response to one antigen that binds better to a different antigen.

HIV—Human immunodeficiency virus, the cause of AIDS.

Host—The human, plant, or animal infected by a pathogen.

HSV—Herpes simplex viruses I and II, which cause cold sores and genital herpes, respectively.

Icosahedron—A polyhedron with 20 equal sides; a common shape for virus capsids.

Immortalization—The conversion of a short-lived cell into a long-lived one.

Immune System—The body system that fights infectious disease.

Immunity—The ability to resist disease.

Incubation Period—The time between infection and the appearance of disease symptoms.

Inflammation—The swelling, redness, and pain associated with an infection.

Interferon—A cytokine that interferes with virus replication and activates the immune system.

Intravenous—(intra-VEEN-us) Given directly into a vein.

IVIG—Intravenous Ig (antibody) collected from many blood donors and containing many antibodies to common pathogens.

Jaundice — (JAWN-dis) Skin yellowing caused by damage to the liver.

Kupffer Cell — A phagocytic cell in the spleen and liver that removes old and damaged blood cells.

Latent Infection — A type of virus infection where virus DNA is present in the host cell, but no new viruses are being made.

Leukemia — A "liquid" cancer where tumorous white blood cells circulate in the blood.

Leukocyte — White blood cell.

Lymph Node — An organ that is a collection of immune system cells that filters microbes from the tissues and contains white blood cells that recognize and fight pathogens.

Lymphocyte — A type of white blood cell, a T or B cell.

Lymphoma — A solid tumor of cancerous immune system cells.

Lysosome — An organelle containing enzymes that digest pathogens and large molecules into smaller molecules.

Macrophage — (macro-FAGE) A type of white blood cell that engulfs and kills microbes.

Malignant Tumor — A tumor that is harmful and spreads away from the original site.

Memory Cells — B cells and T cells that have been previously exposed to an antigen and can now respond faster and better to another encounter.

Meningitis — (men-in-JITE-us) An infection of the membranes covering the brain and spinal cord.

Metastisis — The spread of tumor cells to a new location.

MHC — Tissue-typing molecules that present peptide antigens to T cells.

Microbe — (MIKE-robe) An organism too small to be seen without a microscope; a microorganism.

Microbiology — The study of microbes: viruses, bacteria, fungi, and protozoan parasites.

Mitochondria — Cell organelles that produce ATP to store chemical energy.

Glossary

Monocyte—A type of macrophage that is in the blood.

Nasopharyngeal Carcinoma—(nase-oh-fare-in-GEE-al car-sin-oh-ma) A tumor of the back of the nose and the roof of the mouth caused by Epstein-Barr virus.

Natural Killer Cell—A type of immune system cell that recognizes virus-infected cells and kills them.

Neutralizing Antibody—An antibody molecule that blocks binding of viruses to host cells.

Neutrophil—(NEWT-row-fill) A type of white blood cell that engulfs and kills pathogens.

Normal Flora—Microbes that normally live on and in the body without causing disease.

Nucleocapsid—A virus capsid containing its DNA or RNA genome.

Nucleus—An organelle that contains the cell's DNA genetic information.

Oncogene—A gene that is abnormally active in cancer.

Opportunistic Infection—A bacterial or viral infection that rarely causes death in people with healthy immune systems.

Organelle—A small, membrane-enclosed structure in animal and plant cells.

Pathogen—(PATH-oh-jen) A microbe that causes disease.

Peptide—A small piece of a protein molecule that can bind to MHC-1 and be recognized by T cells.

Phagocyte—(FAG-oh-site) A type of white blood cell that engulfs and kills microbes.

Phagocytosis—(fag-oh-sy-TOE-sis) The process of binding, engulfing, and destroying pathogens and dead cells.

Phospholipid—A kind of fat that is found in plasma membranes of host cells and in virus envelopes.

Plasma—The liquid part of the blood. Plasma is serum plus clotting factors.

Plasma Membrane—A lipid membrane that surrounds all cells: human, animal, plant, and bacterial.

Plasmapherisis—(plasma-fur-EE-sis) The process of removing blood from the body and separating the cells from the plasma; the cells are returned to the body.

Polymerase Chain Reaction (PCR)—A procedure that allows one to specifically copy pathogen DNA, so that very small numbers of pathogens can be detected.

Primer—A small piece of pathogen DNA used for PCR.

Proliferation—Rapid cell division that increases cell numbers.

RBC—Red blood cell.

Reactivation—The process by which a latently infected host cell begins to produce new viruses.

Receptor—A cell surface molecule that binds antigen or cytokines (signaling molecules), which results in changes in the cell's behavior.

Ribosome—An organelle that translates the genetic instructions in messenger RNA into protein.

SCID—Severe combined immune deficiency, an inability to produce B and T cells.

Secondary Antibody—An antibody used in the ELISA test for patient antibodies to EBV. Secondary antibodies specifically bind human antibody molecules and are linked with enzyme molecules.

Serum—The liquid remaining after blood has clotted; serum contains antibody molecules.

Sign—See **Disease Sign**

Spike Protein—A protein on the outside of a virus that allows it to bind to and infect a host cell.

Spleen—An organ that is composed of immune system cells. It filters microbes from the blood and contains white blood cells that recognize and fight pathogens.

Glossary

Spore—Thick-walled structures that some bacteria make to survive harsh environmental conditions.

Stem Cell—A type of bone marrow cell that produces all red blood cells and leukocytes.

Sterile—Without any living microbes.

Symptom—See **Disease Symptom**

T Cell—A type of immune system cell that either regulates immune responses (helper T cells) or kills virus-infected cells (cytotoxic T cells).

Tegument—An EBV protein that surrounds the nucleocapsid and is inside the viral envelope.

Titer—The amount of antibody to a particular antigen in the blood.

TMV—Tobacco mosaic virus.

Transformation—A process by which normal cells become cancer cells.

Tumor—A collection of cancer cells.

Vaccine—Harmless form of a pathogen or antigen that induces a protective response by the immune system.

VCA—Virus Capsid Antigen. A person who has been infected with EBV will have antibodies to VCA in their blood.

Vesicle—A bubble inside a cell. A phagocytic vesicle contains microbes that have been engulfed by a phagocyte.

Viral Integration—The process in which the virus DNA becomes part of the host cell DNA.

Virus—(VY-rus) A very small microbe that must live inside animal or plant cells; often causes disease.

Virus Capsid Antigen—A person who has been infected with EBV will have antibodies to VCA in his or her blood.

Virus Neutralization—Antibodies coating virus particles block the viruses from infecting new cells.

Virus Replication—The process of producing more virus particles inside a host cell.

VZV—Varicella-zoster virus, the cause of chicken pox and shingles.

Notes

1.   Peter Radetsky. *The Invisible Invaders: Viruses and the Scientists Who Pursue Them.* (Boston: Little, Brown and Company, 1991). 8.

2.   Case adapted from P. Radetsky. *The Invisible Invaders.*

Bibliography and Further Reading

BOOKS AND ARTICLES

Beck, Raymond W. *A Chronology of Microbiology in Historical Context.* Washington, D.C.: ASM Press, 2000.

Bennett, J.W. and H.J. Pfaff. "Early Biotechnology: The Delft Connection." *ASM News 59* (8) 1993: 410–404.

Brock, T.D. *Milestones in Microbiology: 1546 to 1940.* Washington, D.C.: ASM Press, 1999.

Chung, K-T. and D.H. Ferris. "Martinus Willem Beijerinck (1851-1931) Pioneer of General Microbiology." *ASM News 62* (10) 1996: 539–543.

Clark, W.R. *At War Within: The Double-Edged Sword of Immunity.* New York: Oxford University Press, 1995.

De Kruif, P. *The Microbe Hunters.* New York: Harcourt Brace and Company, 1926.

Garrett, L. *The Coming Plague: Newly Emerging Diseases in a World Out of Balance.* New York: Penguin USA, 1995.

Henig, R.M. *A Dancing Matrix: How Science Confronts Emerging Viruses.* New York: Random House, Inc., 1994.

Oldstone, M. B. A. *Viruses, Plagues and History.* New York: Oxford University Press, 1998.

Radetsky, P. *The Invisible Invaders: Viruses and the Scientists Who Pursue Them.* Boston: Little, Brown and Company, 1991.

Regis, E. *Virus Ground Zero. Stalking the Killer Viruses with the Centers for Disease Control.* New York: Pocket Books, 1996.

WEBSITES

BNF (British Nutrition Foundation) Awards. Denis Burkitt Study Awards. *www.nutrition.org.uk/awards/burkitt.htm*

"Chronic Fatigue Possibly Related to Epstein-Barr Virus—Nevada." *Morbidity and Mortality Weekly Report* May 30, 1986. Vol. 35:350–352. Available at *www.cdc.gov/epo/mmwr/preview/mmwrhtml/00000740.htm*

Interviews with Dr. Denis Burkitt. Oxford University Medical Video Archive. *http://www.brookes.ac.uk/schools/bms/medical/synopses/burkitt1.html*

Bibliography and Further Reading

Levine, A.J., A. Lustig and D.K. Lvov. "Forward: 100 Years of Virology."
http://ag.arizona.edu/~zxiong/plp611/100year1.html

Reynolds, L.A. "Reye's Syndrome"
http://www.thearc.org/faqs/reyes.html

Websites

American Society for Microbiology
www.asmusa.org

Centers for Disease Control and Prevention
www.cdc.gov

Mayo Clinic
www.mayoclinic.com

National Institutes of Health
www.nih.gov

National Institutes of Health,
information about clinical trials
clinicaltrials.gov

National Institute of
Neurological Disorders and Stroke,
Guillain-Barré Syndrome Information
www.ninds.nih.gov/health_and_medical/disorders/gbs.htm

Index

Human Immuno-
deficiency Virus
(HIV), 14, 33, 58,
69, 83, 90, 102
Human Papilloma
Virus (HPV), 91
Hutkin, Elaine, 23
hybridization, 77

IgG antibody, 72, 75
IgM antibody, 72
immortalization, 65
immune system, 8,
10–11, 14, 34, 51,
55–56, 60, 64, 82–83,
99–101, 103
functions, 78, 84–85
organs of, 38
response to EBV,
36–49, 54, 60–63,
66, 93, 102
immunity, 49
incubation period, 50
infection, 42–44, 50,
58, 67, 71–72, 77,
99–101, see also
latent infection
infectious diseases, 6,
88, 100
infectious mononu-
cleosis
causes, 8, 10–11, 23
diagnosis of, 66–77
and EBV, 8–11, 23,
34, 36, 50, 75–78
prevention, 83–85
rare complications,
52–57
signs and symptoms
of, 8–9, 11,
50–59, 78, 85
treatment of, 78–85
typical, 50–52, 83

inflammation, 37–42,
46, 64, 78
influenza (flu), 6, 79,
82, 96
epidemic of, 12, 59
interferons, 41, 63,
83–84
intravenous adminis-
tration of pooled
antibody molecules
(IVIG), 56, 83
Ivanovsky, Dmitry, 15,
17
IVIG. See intravenous
administration of
pooled antibody
molecules

jaundice, 57

Kaposi's sarcoma, 34,
90
"kissing disease." See
infectious mono-
nucleosis
Koch, Robert, 15, 18
Koop, C. Everett, 22
Kupffer cells, 54–56,
92, 98

latent infection, 31,
58–65, 72, see also
infection
latent virus, 49, 102
Leeuwenhoek, Antony
van, 15, 17
Legionnaires' disease, 6
leukemia, 10, 69, 90,
98–99
leukocytes. See white
blood cells
Löffler, Friedrich, 18
Lyme disease, 6

lymph nodes, 31, 36,
38, 42–44, 46,
50–51, 53, 66–67,
71, 77, 100
lymphocytes, 43,
50–52, 63, 66–67,
99–101, 103
atypical, 68–70
lymphoma, 20–21, 90,
99, 102
lysosomes, 25

macrophages, 39–44,
46–48, 53, 56, 59,
66–67, 71
malaria, 6–7, 92–94
malignant tumor, 86
measles, 32, 49, 79
Medawar, Peter, 26
memory cells, 49
meningitis, 6, 54
symptoms, 57
metastasis, 86
MHC-1 complexes, 26,
41–45, 48, 60, 63–64,
67–70, 88, 92, 95,
99
MHC-2 complexes, 26,
43, 46, 48, 63, 68
microbiology, 18
microscope, 51, 66,
68–69
invention of, 7
mitochondria, 25, 81
monkeypox, 14
mono. See infectious
mononucleosis
monocytes, 66–67, 99
mononuclear cells, 9
Monospot test, 71, 75
Montagnier, Luc, 33
multiple sclerosis, 61
mumps, 32, 49, 71, 79

Index

Picture Credits

9: © Mediscan/Visuals Unlimited
11: © Lester V. Bergman/CORBIS
13: © Farrell Grehan/CORBIS
16: © Christine Case/Visuals Unlimited
16: © Harold Fisher/Visuals Unlimited
25: © Dr. Donald Fawcett/VU
26: Lambda Science Artwork
27: Lambda Science Artwork
29: Lambda Science Artwork
30: Lambda Science Artwork
37: © Dr. Donald Fawcett & E. Shelton/VU
38: Lambda Science Artwork
40: © Noelle Nardone
45: Lambda Science Artwork
47: Lambda Science Artwork
48: © Noelle Nardone
52: © Children's Hospital & Medical Center/CORBIS

53: © Mediscan/Visuals Unlimited
61: Lambda Science Artwork
62: Lambda Science Artwork
67: © Gopal Murti/Visuals Unlimited
70: Lambda Science Artwork
73: © Sid Bloom
73: Lambda Science Artwork
76: Lambda Science Artwork
80: © Science Pictures Ltd./CORBIS
81: Library of Congress
84: Lambda Science Artwork
87: © David Phillips/Visuals Unlimited
89: © Bettmann/CORBIS
93: Lambda Science Artwork
94: Lambda Science Artwork
98: © Ted Spiegel/CORBIS
100: Associated Press, AP

Cover: © Dr. Gopal Murti/Visuals Unlimited

About the Author

Janet Decker grew up in a small town in Michigan planning a nursing career. Then, while in high school, she attended a summer microbiology course sponsored by the University of Michigan and the National Science Foundation. A picture of a virus with its DNA coiled next to it changed her career plans to microbiology.

Dr. Decker received her B.S. in microbiology from the University of Michigan in 1968 and her Ph.D. from UCLA in 1974. She was a National Multiple Sclerosis Society Postdoctoral Fellow at the Walter and Eliza Hall Institute for Medical Research in Melbourne, Australia, and continued her research in immunology at the Frederick Cancer Research Center at Fort Detrick, Maryland, and the Medical University of South Carolina in Charleston. She currently teaches immunology and microbiology as a senior lecturer in the Department of Veterinary Science and Microbiology at the University of Arizona.

Dr. Decker is the author of scientific papers in the field of immunology, of the review text *Introduction to Immunology* published by Blackwell Science in 2000, and of the *Anthrax* volume in this series. She lives in Tucson, Arizona, with her husband, who does research on autoimmune diabetes, and her teenage daughter.

About the Editor

The late I. Edward Alcamo was a Distinguished Teaching Professor of Microbiology at the State University of New York at Farmingdale. Alcamo studied biology at Iona College in New York and earned his M.S. and Ph.D. degrees in microbiology at St. John's University, also in New York. He had taught at Farmingdale for more than 30 years. In 2000, Alcamo won the Carski Award for Distinguished Teaching in Microbiology, the highest honor for microbiology teachers in the United States. He was a member of the American Society for Microbiology, the National Association of Biology Teachers, and the American Medical Writers Association. Alcamo wrote numerous books on the subjects of microbiology, AIDS, and DNA technology as well as the award-winning textbook *Fundamentals of Microbiology*, now in its sixth edition.